IN MINOR AND IN MAJOR:

SUCH IS MY LIFE IN
THE PAYS D'OC

IN MINOR AND IN MAJOR:
SUCH IS MY LIFE IN
THE PAYS D'OC

MARTHE BOYER-BÉLET

Translated by
Julia Wollen

JANUS PUBLISHING COMPANY
London, England

Originally published in French as
en mineur et en majeur
by Les Presses Littéraires, Saint-Estève, 1995
and © Marthe Boyer-Bélet, 1995

First published in English
by Janus Publishing Company 1997
In Minor and in Major:
Such is My Life in the Pays d'Oc

English translation
Copyright © Julia Wollen 1997

British Library Cataloguing-in-Publication Data.
A catalogue record for this book is available from the British Library.

ISBN 1 85756 322 0

Cover design Nick Eagleton

Photoset by Keyboard Services, Luton
Printed and bound in England by
Antony Rowe Ltd
Chippenham, Wiltshire

To my children
To my grandchildren

'Le temps est court qui va de la vigne au pressoir
De l'aube au jour qui baisse.'

Anna de Noailles

(Brief is the time between the vine and the winepress,
From dawn to the darkening of the day.)

Contents

Preface

The story which Marthe Boyer-Bélet tells us here is more than just an autobiographical tale. Certainly this aspect is continually present in the work, initially written for her children and grandchildren, and the passion which she has always brought to everything, the joys and sorrows of a rich experience all find their place at length here. But this book is equally a precious testimony of village life, the life in the villages of the winegrowing Languedoc plain throughout the 20th century. Even though viticulture is not the main subject of this book, it forms the indispensable background to the understanding of this story. Indeed the cultivation of the vine engenders a distinctive kind of existence which makes of winegrowers more craftsmen than peasants, makes the world of wine growing enter the market economy, and introduces into a rural environment the characteristics of an urban mentality. It is this kind of society with its strong identity that Marthe Boyer-Bélet brings to life for us, from the days just after the First World War until our own time. Her personal account, precious to history particularly in relation to social and cultural aspects of village life, is written in clear and unaffected language which makes it a particular pleasure to read.

Jean Sagnes
Professor of Modern History
Président de l'Université de Perpignan

Introduction

When I tell her about my childhood and adolescence, my daughter Mireille is so astonished that she asks me to put it in writing with the intention of handing it down to the family.

I did not comply with her wish immediately, but when I went through a time of loneliness, I felt the need to look back into my past, and in talking about them, thus assuage the loss of all those I had loved.

I think I went beyond what my daughter wanted. Swept along by my enthusiasm, I retraced my life including some very personal details which possibly will shock, but I could not talk about myself and not mention the most important things.

Written records have helped me: a staggering number of letters, all of them interesting, spanning the years between 1914 and 1964. I recognise the rare value of these pieces of writing, telling of parts of people's lives in which each is revealed in a very personal way.

Did I have the right to unearth the copious correspondence of my father during the 'Great War'? I had some reservations about this, for I lifted a veil on the privacy of my parents' marriage, but I cannot pretend not to be pleased at what I found out.

All the other letters, sent to me by various correspondents, relations, my husband, children and friends, have proved to me how much I have been loved, and I owe a deep gratitude to life, and to those round about me and to people I have met.

I hope that the story of my life will interest my family, and perhaps some of them will be surprised by what they find... The youngest ones will have a light shed on their origins and on the way in which we led our lives; mistakes were made, there were some successes, and the whole I find positive, sustained by a faith in existence and a great enthusiasm for others.

My dear children, I dedicate this to you, with all my affection, and do not grieve when I am no longer here. Know that all the joy it is possible to have was mine through the great power of love.

Reflections at the Foot
of a Cedar Tree
(In the guise of a Prologue)

Andante

It is an evening towards the end of November ... the sun is low in the sky, the north wind blows strongly, the last leaves of the chestnut tree fall reluctantly and are mercilessly tumbled along the ground, the branches of the cedar creak and send me desperate messages. I clasp my hands imploring the beautiful tree to bear up against the gale. It was surely pretentious to have planted it there, in our tiny garden; it was placed in the middle of the lawn when my granddaughter Florence was a year old and they were the same height. It has been kind enough to grow as if it were in a beautiful park. During the last few years, we have decorated it at Christmas with garlands and lights; next, a ladder was needed to fix the star to the top ... and now, its tip is higher than the houses and it can look over and observe the traffic in the next street.

From my chair, through the verandah windows, its height reminds me inexorably of the passage of the years; as it has grown, so have we; as it has struggled and faced storms, we have too; like the tree, we have not given in to the decay of the seasonal cycle and have preserved a freshness of soul and generosity of heart.

Now it and I are the only guardians of the house... In thinking of those who are no longer here, of those who saw it grow and of those who never knew it, I remember the whole of my life; a life seems long and yet it is so short; it spins out through one's fingers and I am amazed already to have lived so many years and to have reached the end of the road when I have so many to love and so much to do.

A Peaceful Childhood at the Foot of the Monts Ramus

Overture

1

'It's a girl.' Not such a resounding announcement as might have greeted the arrival of a boy, but I think I was welcomed with joy. So thus I opened my eyes on the world on a spring day in 1912, with nature celebrating, in an unpretentious home, warmed by the love of a couple who had long wanted each other. For various reasons, they were married late at 32 years old, and I was born a year later.

What was she to be called? 'Marthe', my mother hastened to say, in order to stop my father from following up the idea he had conceived during her pregnancy; his choice had alighted on 'Eglantine', a name more in tune with his 'progressive' ideas. Mother, according to the methods of the time, had been delivered by a rather rough midwife of the village, and I assume that it did not all go without a fuss, for my mother, although a courageous person, was extra sensitive to physical pain.

So thus was I entered in the register at the *mairie*, 'daughter of Ernest Boyer, wine-grower, and of Antonia Dijoux, 'without profession', in the pleasant village of Saint-Thibéry, watered by the river Hérault, proudly possessing the vestiges of a Roman bridge and the remains of an extinct volcano pompously entitled 'Monts Ramus'.

My father was the eldest son of Philémon Boyer and Philomène Vidal. What capricious chance caused these two similar names to meet up even though they did not live in the same place? Grandfather was one of the many members of the Canet family near Clermont l'Hérault and grandmother belonged to a middle-class family from Saint-Thibéry.

In this village, grandfather's eldest brother, Léon Boyer, combined the functions of primary school teacher and healer.

Many elderly people tell me of the relief he brought to them thanks to a simple steeping in wine and alcohol and ointments based on a foundation of beeswax.

Surely this presence in the village was the reason for the meeting between Philémon and Philomène, who, though very different, became a very united couple living to a ripe old age.

They enjoyed a robust health: Philémon was a hale and hearty *vigneron* without any intellectual affinity: his fresh face bore a fine white moustache; all the men wore one at that time and I remember the feeling I had when one of my neighbours shaved his off; I no longer dared to look at him, finding the hairless face obscene.

Grandfather's activity was confined to work with the vines and he made his two sons take part in it as well, in spite of their brilliant scholastic results. In 1930 he was proud to be the second person in the village to receive a pension; his pension from the war in 1870 was allocated to him at the rate of 100 francs a month.

Like most of the adults in the village, his conversational speech was in the local dialect which has similarities with Occitan. At the time I rather scorned this language, which the young people did not go in for, and it was only much later that I discovered all its savour.

I cannot resist the pleasure of listing a few of the words, the sounds of which conjure up so well a feeling or condition:

pegosa: something sticking unpleasantly to the fingers
s'esclafar: crushing noisily
afastigos: food which is difficult to eat and digest
se rosegar: to be very anxious without appearing so
plan planet: taking one's time

The Occitan language is so rich that it needs circumlocution to translate one word of it. Almost all the words have an onomatopoeic quality.

* * *

Grandmother, informally called Vidalette, was cultured and used to write faultlessly. Plump, with her still-black hair coiled round her head, framing her face with its sagging cheeks, but without a single wrinkle, she had a serene and contented air. I never saw her look worried or cross. She brought up three children, two boys, Ernest and Auguste, and a daughter Jeanne, who all settled in the village and gave her nine grandchildren.

Family opinion of her differs, but I never heard her speak unkindly to anyone. She accepted life as it was, and people as they were, philosophically.

At the time that I knew my grandparents they were all smiles and indulgence, but they were very severe to their children, even to the extent of forbidding them to have second helpings at table; they insisted upon being addressed as *'vous'* by them. My father, who wanted me to feel closer to them, asked me to *'tutoie'* them, and I ask myself whether they accepted it without annoyance; at any rate they never let it show.

As far as I was concerned, they were an exceptional old couple, leading a calm and steady life in a bourgeois house which seemed very grand to me because of its large balcony which looked out over the road.

Every month, on a Thursday, I went with my mother to give their house a good cleaning. Grandfather found this too much; Grandmother accepted our intrusion, but we respected the attractive disarray on her shelves which were covered with valueless knick-knacks.

I would often go and visit her on my own, and she enchanted me with her stories and songs; I would often ask for the adventures of Dame Tartine which made my mouth water; she would give me a chocolate which had lost its colour from a long stay in the cupboard, and, in spite of its acrid taste I would eat it without batting an eyelid.

Raising my voice because she was extremely deaf, I would tell her the minute details of my schoolgirl doings, at the same time threading a series of needles for her little sewing tasks. Sunday was a good day for them and broke the monotony of the week:

Philémon exchanged his velvet jacket for dark Sunday clothes and put on a large felt hat, while Vidalette donned her beautiful black dress, stiffened with use, and her crêpe bonnet, tying the strings of it under her chin. Thus attired, off they went to mass, leaning on each other. They knew that the *pot-au-feu* was simmering slowly in front of the wood fire, and they accompanied this *bouilli* with an aromatic home-made tomato sauce; the evening meal invariably consisted of *cassoulet* lovingly cooked with vegetables, with their daily kilo of bread. I am still amazed at the capacity of their stomachs.

They never missed a religious office; Grandfather was cantor in the church and he filled the vaults with his powerful voice.

In summer we would go and 'take the air' in front of their house; the folding chairs were brought out from the cellar, and Grandfather would quench our thirst with *anisette* and cool water from the wells.

On Sundays, Grandmother would entertain herself by counting the motor cars going along the road, terrified by the number of them, often fewer than twenty.

Grandfather died suddenly, aged 90, at the beginning of the war.

Philomène came and spent a few months at Capestang, gaining happiness from my little Remi who showered her with love. I would have liked to keep her with us, but I had to resign myself to accept the custom which dictated her staying in turn with each of her three children. Perhaps she was happy to find herself back in the setting of her own village, even in houses which were not her own, and it was while staying with her daughter Jeanne that she died peacefully, set free from a life which no longer held any attraction for her without her companion.

* * *

My maternal grandparents led a less easy life: Mother was the second daughter of Joseph Dijoux and Marie Trumel. They were of unpretentious origins; Great-Grandfather, nicknamed 'le Bordelais' because of his birthplace, inspired the following local epithet through his physical appearance: 'Los bordalesses son seques coma de lenha' (the Bordelais are as dry as firewood).

Grandfather Dijoux was a carter, leaving home early and returning very late. Mother used to tell me that with her mother and sister, in order to calm their anxiety, they would go at about ten o'clock at night to the road on which he would return, and put their ears to the ground to try and hear the trundling of the cart ... one must realise that night-time traffic was scarce in those days.

He was a very gentle and unobtrusive man; Mother never ceased to speak in praise of his kindness, and found it very unjust that he should have such a distressing end to his life; a stroke destroyed his speech and his sight, and he became insane; his daughters looked after him at home and had some very difficult times coping with his strange behaviour.

Grandmother had a thin, stern face; she was never still, her feet treadling away at the sewing machine while she guided the material underneath the presser-foot; she always had work to finish for customers. Working at home as a dress-maker, she made shirts and trousers and did mending in the middle-class homes; ladies' underwear used to be intricate, embellished with little tucks, embroidery and lace. Knickers were long, ending in flounces, and open at the crotch which made it convenient for urinating while standing with out-spread legs. There were some old grannies who didn't manage to do this, and being in their vicinity was most unpleasant. The only luxury that Grandmother had was a long silver chain on which hung her scissors. She used to use a great amount of *fil-chinois*, renowned for its strength, and we would collect up the bits for a little present.

She was worn out by the work, and at the end of her life her health needed constant care. To supplement her diet, meat balls would be added to her soup; I used to steal some of these as I was particularly fond of them. I remember that my mother or my aunt used to walk to Pézénas, seven kilometres from our home, in order to bring back bananas for her – luxury fruit which were not sold in the village.

Both pairs of grandparents were very much a part of my childhood. I used to go to see them often, but my motives were different in each case. The rounded, serene appearance of Vidalette and her warm touch reassured me, and I used to feel a rush of pity for the gloomy emaciated face of Grandmother Dijoux; the prominent veins on her hands distressed me, and I would stroke them, hoping to make them less swollen.

It was she who left us first, and was my first experience of

7

seeing a dead person: under a gauze drape, a stiff black form on a white sheet, a rosary wound round her clasped hands ... the rigid face frightened me. The mirrors in the house had been shrouded under large white sheets, and all day long an uninterrupted file of people passed through, sprinkling the lifeless body with holy water on a branch of sweet bay, while repeating *'elle a payé ... nous, nous devons'* (she has paid the price, we still must). I was nine years old; these words intrigued me: we must what? to whom? I still ask myself the question. At the invitation of one of the members of the family, I kissed the dead forehead, and for a long time afterwards felt the icy touch on my lips.

Mourning dress was very spectacular in those days: black was worn from head to foot and a hat with a crêpe veil, the length of which gradually became less. For a year, full mourning was *de rigueur*, then one entered into *demi-deuil* when one was allowed to wear black and white, grey or mauve. All this involved much extra expense. Naturally, these clothes were accompanied by a restricted social life, particularly for the women; even with the collars of their jackets banded with black crêpe the men had a certain outward freedom. I have always been against these superficial practices from which people did not dare to escape; the colour of one's clothing does not determine the depth of one's grief.

Even though I have never changed my garb, my dear departed ones are always in my heart; I never tire of bringing them to life around me, and while I am still here, they will live for ever.

* * *

I cannot bring my father to mind without emotion, for I admired him unconditionally and always placed him on a pedestal. He loved frankness above all else and used to say to me: 'Daughter, always speak the truth; you will sometimes suffer for it, but you will be at peace with your conscience.' I think I have always honoured this advice; in any event, I was always very upset when I found that someone close to me had lied to me.

He hated dishonest dealings and was indignant at unfairness; his refusal to compromise made him appear eccentric.

He had an intense love of his family and acted as a regular link with the only female relative who did not live in the village and with whom he kept up a regular correspondence; it was always to us that she would come for support when she was in Saint-Thibéry. He was a loyal person who concealed a great sensitivity beneath a rather cool exterior. He never paid me a compliment, but I knew, after his premature death, that he was proud of me and of my academic successes. I regret all the conversations we might have been able to have together, all the valuable things he would have been able to pass on to me, had he been more approachable, and had I had more self-confidence.

He had a lively written style; it revealed a culture gained from solitary study which he did after he left school prematurely at the order of his father and in spite of objections from his teacher. He secretly provided himself with books on various subjects, made himself solve problems and develop literary themes. He must have overcome his father's opposition to have had an old table placed in his bedroom; at this makeshift desk, by the dim light of a candle, he discovered the authors, in little blue books costing a few *centimes* and crudely printed on dreadful paper. The thirst for learning was adjusted to his slender means.

He adored music which he sight-read with astonishing ease and played around with changing keys. He received a collection of works for use by a leader of a wind ensemble; going off on his own to work it out, without the help of an instrument, he sang all the different parts, and when Mother heard his falsetto soaring to imitate the clarinets, she would say, making fun, of him: *'Ausis-lo! Va s'escana!'* ((Listen to him! He'll suffocate!)

He used to play the tuba which gave us some extra income, as he would enliven the dances in the neighbouring villages, to which he would go on foot. Not being an athletic sort, he did not ride a bicycle, and showed little tolerance towards those who practised sport and neglected the arts. He gathered many pupils and also taught music as an 'additional subject', though he was irritated that it was considered of minor importance.

Given the leadership of the local musical society, the Lyre

9

Saint-Thibérienne, he devoted himself unreservedly and unflinchingly to this popular art form for many years. His role as conductor meant that I could take part in the concerts which were given for the musicians on the occasion of their marriage – there were two reasons why this was such an attraction for me:

The 'nightingale's polka' was embellished with trills produced by blowing into a little china object shaped like a bird and filled with water. In addition, I was treated to delicious little cakes, unknown in our home, and I delighted in their melting flavour. I thought all the brides looked strange under their coronets of orange blossom, and I was bewildered by the euphoric atmosphere which surrounded them.

My father entered his musical society for many competitions, and brought back some dazzling prizes: at the competition in Sceaux, the jury was headed by Marc Delmas, winner of the prix de Rome, and on the death of this composer, the local newspaper *Le Petit Méridional* printed on 7th December 1931:

La Lyre Saint-Thibérienne will always keep in its heart the memory of the master's generous praise, the many and magnificent awards which he bestowed on it, and the congratulations which he gave publicly to its conductor with so much warmth and sincerity.

Actually, Father told me that what Delmas had said in front of all the societies concerned was: 'This conductor has the reddened hands of a peasant; he doesn't wear cuffs, but he's a great musician.' He had been very touched by this tribute.

During the 'Great War' of 1914–18 my father was recruited into the territorial army in Morocco. He was sheltered from the murderous perils of the front line; on the other hand, he suffered greatly from the imposed long separation from his family, broken only by very rare home leaves.

I discovered the daily letters which he sent my mother at this time, and I read his warm and lively epistles with joy and deep emotion; his small, fine writing covers 1700 sheets of paper, on which he expresses his hatred of the war, his sadness at being deprived of his child growing up so far away from him, his concern for our health and well-being. The letters are a record of the life in that colony at the beginning of the century, the customs of the indigenous people, the strict demands of certain army officers, the hospitality of the colonial families, and tales of various plagues, such as the onslaught of locusts which brought everything to a stand-still!

From these letters I learnt that my life might have taken a very different turn if Mother had agreed to join him in Meknès where he was offered the post of musical director.

What marvellous power there is in the written word, to preserve all the thrills of a lifetime, all the happenings of an era; nowadays the telephone diminishes this precious inheritance.

Postcards which were for me, accompanied the letters, expressing the hope of a speedy return; alas to be disappointed:

> I wish August would pass quickly, and the end of the month will find us together again, then the kisses will be better than the ones I have been sending you these past two years, and those which get lost in space when you send them to me, however sweetly, on the tips of your pretty fingers.

and later on, a father's tender pride!

> Life, my angel, which will surely smile upon you and bring you to a time of precious love, will teach you that nothing counts nor lasts more than the good wishes you send for your papa's return. What more can I ask of such a little girl when she knows how to spread joy and happiness wherever she goes and in all she does for a papa in exile, what sweeter satisfaction, than to receive so many good marks. I am thankful for all the happiness that you give. Though we are far apart, the joy that you spread about you enters my heart which is always close to yours and to your darling mother whom I embrace in you and with you.

11

I was a very little girl, just six years old, when my father came back, and it was only much later that I discovered, with emotion, all his love for me.

He used to exchange news with his parents and his other conscripted friends, especially with his brother Auguste who experienced the discomfort and terror of life in the trenches, and who, together with his brother-in-law Raoul, was exposed to the dangers of the front. His long-standing friendship with the *deputé* Barthe, quaestor to the Chamber of Deputies, gave him access to valuable information on the political life of the country, international relations, and decisions affecting wine production relevant to our area.

During the conflict, a generous person in Saint-Thibéry had a bright idea. To keep up the morale of the *poilus* of his village, he edited a paper called *Le Patelin* which gave an account of the little happenings of our town; each week, in all the nerve centres of the war and even overseas, the soldiers avidly read this little local bulletin.

While she was on her way to do the spraying, Mademoiselle Célestine Barabès saw a baby hare and chased after it like a gazelle; she was delighted to catch it and take it back alive to her home where she is bringing it up on a bottle.

Mademoiselle Blanche, on her way from getting the bread, was nibbling away at it while walking along the street, when a woman said to her: 'L'accabes pas tout' (don't finish it all); as she said this, she tripped up, and Blanche replied: 'E bas, fagues atenciou de pas tomba' (and you, watch out you don't fall over); having thus replied, she herself fell full length on the cobblestones.

It was simple fun, but it was life from their far off village! A soldier from Saint-Thibéry wrote this poem:

Le Patelin pour nous est un peu du foyer
Un lambeau detaché d'un petit coin de France
Ou se trouvent tous ceux à qui le soir l'on pense
Avec des cauchemars que l'on ne peut noyer

Il vient de Cessero* que nous devons défendre
Et grâce au cher Mathieu dont le devoir est tendre
It chasse le cafard, met tant de baume aux coeurs
Que les plus attristés prennent des airs rieurs

O papierou langut, ambé tas galjadas
Semènos a brassat de boneur dins las tranchadas
Malgré mon affectioun per tan qué te desiré
Soueti souben ta mort per finir moun martyre.

(Le Patelin is a bit of home for us
A fragment of a little part of France
Where live all those we think of in the evening,
And dream about in nightmares without cease.

It comes from Cessero which we must defend,
And thanks to dear Mathieu and his loving task,
It drives away the blues, brings cheer to our hearts,
That even the saddest of us may raise a smile.

You chatty little paper, with your jokes,
You spread your happiness in handfuls in the trenches,
However much I love and long for you,
I often wish you no more which would mean I could
    return.)

The little paper, printed with a very rudimentary stencilling machine, also published a list of soldiers on leave, wounded comrades, those taken prisoner and those killed in the field of honour.

In addition, Mathieu had created a little museum out of some premises in the village, and there were displayed all the trophies and souvenirs sent from the front by the troops. It was open every Sunday and it was there that celebratory bottles were uncorked in honour of someone home on leave. Evidence of a generosity which deserves to be put on record.

* Cessero: the ancient name for Saint-Thibéry

My father's altruism and his wish to improve the lot of the workers quickly pushed him into militant action. He and his brother-in-law Raoul worked very effectually in the socialist party. He remained unmarried for a long time and incurred the wrath of his father who held opposing views; but this did not diminish the son's affection nor respect.

He continued his entirely voluntary musical and political activities with the same enthusiasm after his marriage to Antonia Dijoux, who was, according to her eldest sister Emilie (not renowned for her compliments), one of the prettiest girls in the village. She had been taught at a convent and had not had a very broad education. The things she remembered most from it were the simple plays that she had performed and one of the songs which she still used to sing to us in her final years and which depicted her very much as she was when she grew older:

Quand j'avais quinze ans
J'étais bien aussi folle qu'elle
Et de mes trente deux dents
Je riais et j'étais très belle
J'ai perdu ma beauté
Mais mon rire est resté
Et si ma bouche est incomplète
Je me console quand je répète
Se resouvenir, c'est apprendre a vieillir.

(When I was fifteen
I was just as wild as she is
And with all my thirty-two teeth
I used to laugh and was so beautiful.
I have lost my beauty
But my laughter is still there
And if my mouth is empty
I console myself when I repeat
That to go over old memories is to learn how to grow
   old.)

As a young girl she worked in a sewing workshop which resounded with laughter and song; I imagine that as she plied her needle, a song on her lips, she would dream of her loved one, waiting patiently for him to finish his union business before he would ask to marry her.

She often went to stay at Montpellier with her mother's sister, whose son, Arthur, was a printer; the outings in the town, and to the theatre in the inexpensive seats filled her with joy, and her aunt was delighted to accompany her attractively dressed niece, for my grandmother took great pains over the outfits of her daughters: full, long dresses, made of beautiful material and decorated with ribbons, braids, flounces and lace, wide-brimmed hats, covered with flowers or even birds ... long leather gloves covering the arms up to the elbows.

These garments kept their bodies concealed from their chins to the tips of their boots. I have discovered how this sumptuous way of dressing looked from old photographs, for I have no personal memories of my mother as a young woman: her hair turned white early, and because of successive periods of mourning I always saw her dressed in black: she never allowed herself to dream or escape into fantasy, and I was happy to know that by marrying late, she was able to prolong the pleasures of adolescence and of helping her sister Emilie, mother of three children.

At 18, she enjoyed having a niece with whom to share much of her life. They had a close relationship to the end and Mother would often mix up our two names, calling me Anne for example, which used to irritate me slightly.

After her marriage, she lived in the shadow of her committed champion of the people; she relished simple pleasures: surrounding herself with her beloved sister's children and maintaining her regular attendance at church which she never neglected to do so long as her health allowed.

I experienced her as always being unwell, frequently complaining of what she called her *'douleurs'* which used to keep her in bed for several days; my childhood was disrupted by her crises. At these times my father and I would eat together on our own; he used to refuse any help in preparing the meal, and I used to hold back my tears while listening to the long moans of my mother; I remember my disappointment when, thinking to divert her with a story which I liked very much,

15

she swiftly sent me out of the room, and I felt very angry to have been treated so unfairly.

Her thinness frightened me, and I was often afraid that she was going to die prematurely. Her slight body, so sensitive to pain, did not let her down and she was with me until I retired, whereas, against all expectations, it was my father who was taken from me in the middle of my adolescence.

II

Situated in a busy shopping street, our home was unpretentious, but I used to call it 'the pretty house'.

The ground floor consisted of one room, and had a concrete
floor; the stairs and the upper floor had red floor-tiles which
my mother used to get down on her knees to polish.

The most attractive room was the bedroom which I used to
share with my parents: the furniture, bedecked with mirrors
and columns, made a great impression on me. It was, according to tradition, my parents' wedding present from their two
families. What pleasant nights I spent in the reassuring
nearness of my father and mother, in the dim glow of the
'Pigeon' lamp which kept alight until morning. It was there,
one Thursday, that I disposed of my purgative, between the
wall and my cot. I still feel sickened when I think of that
regular, inflicted torture. We weren't given vitamins in those
days, but every spring, a purgative was the accepted remedy,
to 'cleanse the blood': either castor oil or magnesium salts, it
didn't matter which. The two were equally disgusting, as was
the daily dose of cod-liver oil.

We also had the room which was called the 'de toilette', in
which the only furniture was a table on which stood a basin, a
jug, and the necessary things for doing one's hair. It was there
that de-lousing took place; like every child, I picked up lice at
school, and on Wednesday evenings, my mother, having
sprinkled my hair with a black powder, *la cibadille*, tied it up
tightly in a cap; this hurt intensely all through the night, and
the next day a very brisk washing eliminated the 'victims'. I
dreaded this unpleasant treatment, but, thanks to it, my hair
was washed from time to time; the idea of a weekly shampoo
was not yet a habit. Not a single household in the village had a

17

shower. In the summer we sometimes had a soak in a copper, which was filled with water and then allowed to warm in the sun.

Adjoining the upstairs rooms was a large attic, almost empty, but full of mystery for me. I used to imagine that the cats and mice from La Fontaine's fables lived among the few bags that were stored there.

I was a placid child; it could have been somewhere else, but I can see myself in the large kitchen, doing my homework on the table, or going over my lessons in my mind, while in the same room, my father would be teaching musical theory or the playing of wind instruments to three young men; my mother would be knitting in a corner and taking care not to move during the class. In winter we would be illuminated by the oil lamp, and its wick would be turned up from time to time to increase the circle of light. After the meal there was not much left of the evening: my father taught me the usual parlour games, and I suspect that he often cheated because I used to win a little too often. The summer evenings were spent outside the front door, where all the neighbours brought out their chairs, and the peace and quiet, and the mildness of the evening would be shared in happy conversation until a late hour. The men used to make jokes which I could not understand, but which made me feel slightly ill at ease. It was in this house that I was rocked to the sound of Occitan songs, hypnotically sending one to sleep.

> Som, som, som,
> Venis, venis, venis
> Som, som, som,
> Venis, venis donc.
> Le som vol pas venir
> La pichona vol pas dormir
> Som, som, venis, etc . . .

(Come, sleep, sleep doesn't want to come – the little one doesn't want to sleep – Sleep, sleep come, . . .)

To punctuate my first steps, and holding the end of my pinafore in her hand, my mother used to sing:

Auça lo mantal,
Roquetona, Roquetona,
Auça lo mantal,
Roquetona, un pauc pus naut

(Lift up your pinafore, Roquetona, lift it up, Roquetona, a little higher.)

We rented 'the pretty house'; in 1921 my parents were able to realise their ambition of owning their own home; it was a lucky find. Our new house was well situated in a quiet and pleasant area. The accommodation over the *cave* looked out onto countryside for as far as the eye could see; as the railway line bordered our little garden, the view was crossed regularly by the passage of trains.

The balconies outside the windows, the decorated iron front door surmounted with a fanlight on which were entwined my father's initials, the large grey stone staircase up which were forged-iron banisters which ended in a cut-glass ball – all appeared to me to be great luxuries compared to the simplicity of my previous home; and besides, we had the rare privilege of a dining-room; the furniture was simple, but a pink marble fireplace over which hung a large mirror gave a definite splendour.

Next to the spacious, sunny kitchen, always soberly adorned with the Post Office calendar, was a store-room, the *souillarde*, where we hung the home-cured *cochonailles* and the grapes which were eaten in the winter; the stocks of the bars of Marseilles soap dried out there on a shelf.

The charming appearance of this house inspired my mother to make some efforts at decoration – embroidered curtains at the windows, covers and mats on the furniture, pictures on the walls. I used to gaze with admiration at the conductor's diploma awarded to my father at the Biarritz festival, which depicted Bizet conjuring up his compositions: the great musician, seated at the piano, seemed captivated by the provocative glance of the comely Carmen, while in the corner of the picture was the unobtrusive silhouette of the Girl from Arles. Did my subconscious even then register the desire to interpret his works?

In our new house we had two important bonuses, little

known in the villages in those days: electricity and running water. At the simple touch of a porcelain button, the light blazed forth, illuminating all the nooks and crannies; to us it seemed magical. The dining-room was lavishly lit by four bulbs which surrounded the hanging light-fitting, under an opaline shade.

My mother was relieved to have finished with the drudgery of water-collecting; we now had a tap in the cellar and in the sink, and we were thrilled with this uninterrupted flow which ensured a supply for so many of our needs.

A well gave us cool water to drink in the summer, and we kept certain foodstuffs in a metal basket which hung above the water on a rope.

The houses of those days were far from being endowed with the comfort and charm that we enjoy today; the rooms were not brightened up with indoor plants; only a pot of basil would be given room on the window-sill as it had the reputation of keeping insects away. This didn't stop us, in the summer, from having to hang up in the rooms dreadful strips of sticky paper on which the flies gathered to be killed. Around a hole dug out of the earth at the bottom of the garden stood a shack made out of loose planks which served as a lavatory. It was primitive and uncomfortable but one was secluded from prying eyes.

The kitchen was the only room which was heated in the cold season: in the evenings we would gather round the fireplace where a good fire glowed and hold out our hands towards it, with our feet on foot-warmers. As he poked up the fire, my father would send up a burst of sparks, and thus I would lose myself in blissful contemplation, filled with a happy serenity in the security of my home.

When one went to bed, the bedrooms were cold, but in the bed was *le moine*, a utensil in which was suspended a pot full of glowing embers which made a hump under the bedclothes. It was taken out, and one snuggled down in the warmth which didn't last long. My father, who did not think this procedure was very healthy, preferred to trail over my sheets the copper warming pan which has now become a wall decoration.

Later on, we used a hot brick wrapped in newspaper.

Happily the beds had goose-down quilts which spread a light and gentle warmth.

I enjoyed the warmth of these evenings at home, and accepted reluctantly – without letting it show – having to go twice a week to spend the evening with my grandmother. On Tuesdays and Fridays my father would go and rehearse his musicians, and at my mother's request he used to accompany us as far as the convent square. It was often cold; I was wrapped up in a large shawl so that I could only half see out of it, and off we went together, both of us hanging on to my father's arms while he guided us along the dark streets.

Underneath our living quarters was a vast *cave* for all the wine-making equipment: a wooden cask in which the wine was matured, a wine press and a cement vat, and a range of barrels in which were improved the fine wines carefully developed by my father. In a dark corner was the bedding for our donkey, Pompon, who was so useful to my father, carrying him along in the vines in his little cart. He often used to make the floor of our house reverberate with his loud brays. Despite the gentleness of his big eyes, he was strong-willed, and would not tolerate taking orders from women: one day, my aunt Emilie wanted to use him to go to Pézénas: my father harnessed up Pompon; my aunt, without showing herself, got into the cart discreetly and off they went. All went well until, sensing the speed slackening, my aunt pulling on the reins, unwisely called out 'Allez-hue, Pompon.' At the sound of her voice, our donkey lay down on the road: an obliging passer-by had to make him get up and lead him back to the stable.

In summer, we used to install ourselves on the bottom floor to benefit from the cool of the *cave* during the very hot months: my father fixed up a cupboard to house the crockery, and my mother cooked on a little charcoal stove in the hearth: we used to eat our meals on the folding laundry table which we took out into the garden in the shade of a large pear tree: the salad would be soaking in the bucket full of cold water, and I would shake it out in the wire basket which was designed for the purpose. I sometimes use it still, to the great delight of my granddaughters, who declare, poetically, that I am 'making the leaves dance' . . .

Like us, our neighbours came down into their garden, which nothing separated from ours, and we would eat side by side, in an atmosphere of conviviality. I used to enjoy this unusual arrangement, and the unaccustomed ambiance imparted all the feeling of a holiday, which was something we never gave ourselves...

III

As a child, I was rather slow and shy, blushed easily, and was quick to burst into tears; this must have irritated my mother, who used to say to me teasingly:

> 'Pompez Seigneur, pour les biens de la terre
> Et le repos du militaire.'

(Oh God, pump out the water, for the sake of the earth and the peace of the army.) This used to annoy me intensely.

Although I felt cosily secure in my family, I would sometimes dream of escaping from the confines of my life which I found narrow and hum-drum. I remember the feeling of longing I experienced the day one of my friends came to say goodbye to our teachers. Her father, who was employed by the railway, had been posted to the North, and I envied her going to new surroundings and a new life.

I was very sensitive: to see suffering stayed in my mind a long time, and bird song filled me with excitement. I remember a sense of outrage which was provoked by a wanton act of cruelty; I was 12 at the time; we had gone with my father to visit some friends at Pouget, a village near Clermont l'Hérault. In the public square a group of over-excited children were shrieking with glee: there was a rat trap in the middle of them, encircled with flames, and four terror-stricken creatures were running hither and thither, throwing themselves against the bars. This dreadful scene haunted me for a long time.

* * *

My childhood and adolescence were brightened and supported by the presence of Margot: she was the youngest daughter of my mother's sister, already burdened with a large family. Margot had lost her father who had gone missing in the Great War: after a salvo of gunfire he was never found, and many questions were raised. My valiant aunt Emilie hardened in her grief, lived on with the unresolved questions in her heart, and brought up her four children with dignity, taking in sewing for customers.

Margot and I grew up together, side by side, sharing the same joys and sorrows and the same ailments. Although she was born only two months before me, I thought of her as my elder sister, for she was more responsible and less fanciful than I was. Thanks to her, I experienced the concern and support of a sister and avoided the boredom and selfishness of an only child.

The similarity of our ages and the way we were dressed made us look like twins. We didn't have an extensive wardrobe, but we used to consult each other in order always to be dressed the same. We went to Pézénas for our clothes, seven kilometres from home; we would go there by train, or by cart when my father used to accompany us, and sometimes on foot, stopping half way at Nézignan l'Evèque.

We always bought our material at the maison Maurel; our mothers were anxious to know if someone else in the village had made the same choice: 'For just think, what if we wear something for Sunday best and another person should put it on during the week...?'

Everyone respected the established code of dress: there was the 'go anywhere' dress for the week, Sunday best, and then clothes for special occasions, and one never changed them about ... It was the same in respect of the rhythm of the religious festivals; one wore one's Christmas coat which one exchanged for a suit at Easter, whether the temperature was warmer or not.

Then, we would go to our dressmaker, Madame Lacourt, in a gloomy house which had a beautiful Italianate gallery. For our summer clothes, we would send her surreptitious signals to reduce the length of the sleeves which our mothers insisted should come down to the elbows. Our milliner was Madame Lacourt's pretty niece. We would choose the style, begging her to make two copies exactly the same as each other.

24

A little less often, but regularly all the same, we used to go to the corset-maker; the chest had to be supported, and we were imprisoned in a casing of twill stiffened with rigid whalebones. I had an unfortunate tendency to curvature of the spine: to remedy this I was made to wear strong rubber straps which pulled my shoulders back, leaving red and painful indentations on my skin; this kind of hair shirt didn't help at all.

When I was young, the day-to-day dress of a little girl consisted of a percale shift with straps, or, worse, a corset, knickers of woven or knitted fabric, an undergarment called a *combinaision*, a dress, and a large pinafore. Stockings were knitted in cotton or wool. During the week, to keep from getting cold one wore a cardigan or was wrapped in a large scarf. It was the custom to wear a *cravate*, a wide black ribbon round the neck, and this bad habit was responsible for many colds.

For underwear and household linen, we had recourse to the commercial travellers from the big manufacturers in the Tarn, who visited their customers regularly. They were trustworthy suppliers who brought beautiful cloths, large sheets in linen, or cotton and linen mix, and a variety of articles which stocked up the cupboards of which the housewives were proud.

From the time that I was 12 years old, my mother started collecting my trousseau which she used to embroider in the evenings. Alas, all these finely sewn articles lie idle on the cupboard shelves, ousted by the modern linen of today which is lighter and easier to care for.

* * *

Apart from shopping for clothes, our trips to Pézénas always consisted of the usual round of visits. We were strictly obliged to go and call on the Blanc family, parents-in-law of Anne who was Margot's eldest sister. Their house was in the Place de Poissonerie and had the austere, slightly dismal air of old Pézénas houses. At least, that was how we saw it, for we were so accustomed to the town that we went through it without noticing its treasures; far from appreciating its old doorways, the charm of its narrow alleys and the beauty of carved

25

stairways standing out in the shadow of an entrance, we only noticed the neglected appearance of the squares and the dilapidated state of certain buildings.

It was not until later that I discovered and admired its architectural heritage and the touching imprint of vanished splendour.

Monsieur Blanc's upholsterer's workshop was next door to the Barber Gély of Molière fame.* This seemed nothing out of the ordinary to us. One went down a step to go in, and there our friend, his mouth full of tacks, would tell us amusing stories while re-covering seats, made of velvet and satin, material which reminded us oddly of the outfits on our Christmas dolls. Madame Blanc, a good-looking woman with fair hair, dominated her husband with her height and authority. If we had a little time to spend, we went up an old stone staircase into an immense upstairs room; there the light came in sparsely through the narrow, small-paned windows, but there were always sweetmeats for us ... from the town!

The Escudié ladies, who lived in the house opposite, often wished us to call: this was a refined ambiance where people spoke and expressed themselves in a genteel way; the youngest of the girls, Mariette, had a beautiful, pale face, surrounded by tightly curled brown hair. She seemed to me like a character from a fairy tale.

After a short stop with Mademoiselle Blanc, Anne's aunt, a stylish person with snow-white hair, my aunt used to say: 'We must go and see Madame Michel.' She was a war widow, and her husband had known my uncle during those dreadful times. She lived with her son and his family. The son was a gardener, an occupation which was quite common in Pézénas, where the rich soil was well suited to market gardening. My father used to benefit from his experience and would stock up with garden seedlings from him; he

---

* Barber Gély was a friend of Molière and as well as being a barber, he also made wigs and practised some rudimentary dentistry in his shop (now the Tourist Information Office in Pézénas). Molière used to come and seat himself on a special high-backed chair, particularly on market days when there was lots going on, in order to listen to the gossip and observe the customers, who provided him with some of the ideas and characters for his plays.

valued his advice which revealed a great knowledge of plants: 'Lavez souvent vos plantes d'aubergines, car elles aiment la propreté.' (Wash your growing aubergines often, as they like to be clean.)

We always had a very warm welcome from them and young Madame Michel would fill us to the brim with cakes and chocolate.

Afterwards we would go and collect our donkey which had been left '*à l'affenage*', and, lulled by the movement of the cart, we took the road back to the village, content, and with our heads full of dreams.

Sometimes I used to accompany my father to Béziers when he went to collect payment for the sale of the wine. What an undertaking that was. We caught the train at 8.0 a.m.; the journey seemed very long to me; when we got off at the station, the Plateau des Poètes enchanted me with its banks of boulders and the swans which swam in stately fashion on the ornamental lakes. We always used to make a few purchases at the Magasins Modernes (now the Nouvelles Galeries). It was a different world, and I was impressed with the variety of items on sale. Then my father took me on to the Halles where he bought things which were unobtainable in the village. I was dazed by the clamour, the intensity of the crowds and the mass of varied merchandise.

The town was an unfamiliar world for me. At mid-day we would go and eat at a restaurant; I felt intimidated at being waited on like a lady. I felt more at home in the Café Saint Félix where I would sometimes go with my mother; the food was simple, and we used to meet people from neighbouring villages, with whom we rapidly struck up acquaintance.

These outings were very few and far between; my parents' situation made it necessary for them to be economical; income from winegrowing was uncertain, and my father had the worry of *une année d'avance* as he used to call it. Because of this, devoted as he was to music and the theatre, he would very seldom go to a production in town, and this I greatly regret.

* * *

At the times when our mothers were occupied working in the

vines, we used to take our mid-day meal with Grandmother Dijoux. I especially loved the soups made with our own olive oil, and the flavoursome mackerel *bourrides*. My grandmother's house was very picturesque; perched at the top of three flights of steps, it dominated the Place du Couvent, the lively centre of the village. Behind its narrow façade, three rooms, one on each floor, had little dark cubby holes as extensions. The glazed front door allowed a feeble light into the large kitchen: the wide fireplace spanned the whole width of one wall, and on each side of the hearth, two little chairs were set for us.

Adjoining the kitchen was the *souillard*, where a huge jar of olives spiced with bay and fennel stood imposingly; our hands often strayed into it; this room was provided with a very basic sink – a stone bowl with a hole in it, through which the dirty water flowed into a bucket which had to be emptied frequently. For this chore, luckily there was a sloping garden behind the house; it was covered in wild grasses and opened out onto the countryside; it was a playground to dream about. Subsequently all its magic disappeared with the building of a school complex close by.

One had to go and fetch water from the fountain and carry up heavy pitchers for cooking and household needs.

It often happened that during the meal, an argument would blow up between us about something that had happened at school; we would start to come to blows, pull each other's hair and pinch each other, and after a few tears we would go into fits of giggles which used to annoy our grandmother the most of all.

In spite of her severity, we enjoyed being at her home, and the house, in which Margot lived long afterwards, held a strange attraction for us.

The new owners have modernised it; I have resisted the invitation to go back there, as I do not wish to disturb my fond memories.

When we assembled for shared family evenings together, we were quite a crowd: my cousins Fernand and Justine, their children, my aunt etc ... While the women's fingers wound wool to make into bodices or socks, Margot and I would look after the little ones, singing them nursery rhymes or telling them stories.

28

When they fell asleep in a basket or with their arms folded on the table, we enjoyed re-reading our favourites: 'Grands Coeurs', or samples of books which Margot's sister, a primary school teacher, had brought us.

When we were young, it was down Grandmother's large chimney that le père Noël used to come. After giving the grate a thoroughly good clean, we would place our grandfather's clogs there, and in the morning were thrilled to find a mandarin and a chocolate clog, with the tiniest model of a pink sugar baby Jesus. One year – oh what luxury! – there was a *togne* – a doll, made out of pasteboard, without legs, which my aunt had dressed in such a way that the clothes could not be taken off; from under a dark red velvet bonnet (made of scraps of material from Monsieur Blanc) escaped a few tufts of hair which had been stolen from us.

We were never dissatisfied by the simplicity of our presents, but some parents inflicted disappointment on their children. I remember the year that the children next door found a horse dropping in their clog. What had they done to deserve that?

We didn't put Christmas trees in our houses, and they didn't appear in the village shops. Despite the absence of splendour and decorations, Christmas has always been a favourite festival for me; I love this magical time when the joyful sound of the bells chiming gladdens the heart, and when the family gatherings are so heartwarming.

At home, we never missed celebrating New Year's Eve. With a great deal of care, my father would make the preparations while all the rest of the family, including the cousins, attended the midnight mass: the church seemed quite different then; joyful songs filled the vault:

> Pastres, pastretas, derrevelhatz-vos pecaire,
> Que vostre paire a besonh de vos pecaire
> (Well, shepherds and shepherdesses, awake,
> Well, your father has need of you)

The traditional joy of this special night is more fervently expressed in our Occitan tongue. After the celebration of the mass, we would go towards the crèche, where the stiff faces of the figures frightened us a little, and we would slip a coin in the box held by an angel, to see its head nod several times to thank us.

What a delight it was, after the cold walk home, to find ourselves at the table, which was beautifully laid with a white cloth, by a big, open wood fire: the *plat de résistance* was sausage grilled on the glowing embers, and my father had unhooked the lovingly preserved bunches of grapes.

One year something unfortunate happened. When we got back and were impatient to get in, we found our doorway completely blocked up by a pile of firewood; it took a long time to clear it away.

Next day, we learned that we had been victims of a misunderstanding; the 18-year-old daughter of our neighbours was going to a dance with some young people who wanted to play a joke on her and they had chosen the wrong door. From the floor above, my father had heard nothing.

On New Year's Day I had to go and present my good wishes to all the members of the family and all our friends; I felt this to be a real chore.

No sooner awake, and feeling a bit embarrassed, I would burst in to my parents' bedroom, having knocked discreetly first.

The evening before, I would send my grandparents a letter, most painstakingly written on gold lacy paper with a beautiful relief design ... I remember that each year I used to write the same words: *'leur verte vieillesse'*. The formula must have appealed to me. Before mid-day, I would meet up at their house with all my cousins, the children of uncle Auguste and aunt Jeanne, and Vidalette would open the jar of dates preserved in alcohol; we would each receive our share in a slightly opaque liqueur glass and gallantly swallow down the contents. We would be given an *écu*, which my father always put aside for us. Beforehand I would have visited uncles, aunts, cousins and neighbours. Phew!

IV

My mother's day began invariably with preparing the coffee: with the coffee-mill wedged between her knees, she would turn the handle to grind the beans, then very slowly she would pour little ladles of boiling water over the grounds; it was pleasant to wake up to the lovely smell pricking one's nostrils.

Cooking was done in earthenware or cast-iron pots which would be put in front of a fire made from *souches*. Keeping the fire going needed constant attention, but how delicious those dishes tasted, simmered slowly on the heat of the embers. Our palates have never savoured anything like them since. To heat up breakfast we set light to a *sarment* (in Bas Languedoc a *buche* is a vine shoot, and a *sarment* is a little bunch of vine shoots), and the pot was put on a tripod. Many people used to use a little spirit stove to avoid the unpleasant taste of smoke but my father, fearing accidents, never wanted one. For cooking *ragoûts* we made use of the *potager* adjoining the chimney – an opening with two cavities for the embers and charcoal. Roasts were cooked in the fireplace on a grill, or on a spit which was something we often used at home. At the end of the cooking time, one particular ritual delighted me: from the white-hot *capucin* (a long rod fitted with a little pierced funnel containing lard) fell drops of flaming fat which basted the meat or poultry, made it a golden colour and gave it a delicious flavour.

As for the game birds, for which we had a smaller spit, the thing to do was not to gut them, but to collect the juices on buttered slices of bread placed underneath.

These details go to show that my father was a real gourmet, eating and drinking with discernment, and I almost dare to say, with reverence. Meals were an occasion for the family to be together, and we took our time. The crockery was always just as it should be, and the glasses were of good quality.

The day we bought a stove was a revolution. I can see it now, in green enamel; we took great care of it, for it allowed us to cook better meals: we could make *gratins* and we launched into baking home-made cakes: tarts and madeleines. Its firebox was fed with lumps of charcoal, a stock of which was kept in the *cave*, and we pulled it up in a black bucket specially kept for the purpose.

Previously, we would make use of the baker's oven. One evening I had a misadventure there. Going to collect our meal, I got tangled up in the jute curtain of the shop and I dropped the dish; the contents spilled into the stream. It was a summer evening and the street was very busy. That day at the music rehearsal, my father was asked, teasingly: 'Tell us, Ernest, did the aubergines taste good?' In other days it would have been worthy of a mention in *Le Patelin*.

From time to time, my mother would show me how to cook, but she would never give me the exact proportions of any-thing: 'How much flour should I put in?' 'You'll see how much', she would reply invariably. We had no scales at home, and the ingredients were judged *a bisto de naz* – by guess-work.

For the Carnival festivities, we used to make *oreillettes*. My mother kneaded flour, eggs and butter together, added some yeast, and put the large lump of dough to rise under the warmth of the eiderdown; the next day, my grandmother, aunt and female cousins would come in force, and bits of the dough were stretched very finely; we all had different methods of doing it: my grandmother pulled it tightly round her closed fist, my aunt did it on her knee; nowadays it is done in all directions with a roller. We would toss the dough rings into boiling fat; they would sizzle and swell up, and once drained and sprinkled with sugar, they would be placed carefully in a basket lined with a white cloth. In my youth they used to be cooked on a fire of vine roots, and the person in charge of the cooking, armed with a skimmer at the end of a long stick, would have a bright red face.

The pastries which were eaten at the end of the local *fête repas* were different: these were *tourtes* of such huge dimensions that they could only be cooked in the baker's oven. *Specialists* went from house to house to knead the dough, and fill them with stewed apples or crushed nuts mixed with brown sugar.

The evening before the *fête*, a long queue stretched in front of the bakery; a surreptitious glance measured up the next person's cake; each had its own particular hallmark – ours was always marked with almonds.

In spite of the tempting look of these *tourtes*, one was scarcely able to appreciate a taste of them, as they were served at the end of a lavish meal in which oysters, entrées, cooked dishes, roast meats, game, vegetables and cheese followed one upon another.

Against the dining room wall stood the dust-covered bottles of wine to accompany each dish; these rosés and reds, dry wines, sweet or sparkling, were made by my father, matured in oak barrels, and he would serve them reverently to his guests. He was very reserved, but he was immensely proud of his cellar and the fact that it was well-stocked by his own hands.

There would be many sorts of after-dinner liqueurs: cacao, chartreuse, curaçao, and liqueur de Dantzig in which glittered little golden specks. This was manufactured with extracts of Noirot and alcohol, and we were treated to it by the distillery.

Each family had its guests, and at our table we would often have some musicians from Montblanc, the next-door village, who came to swell the ranks of the local wind band which gave concerts to the public.

Very occasionally we would have ice cream; certain posh wedding banquets would end with a *bombe glacée*; it was made by pouring the cream into a pewter container, which in turn was placed in a wooden barrel full of ice and salt: this was stirred round by a copper paddle, while the inside container was kept revolving with a crank handle.

To quench our thirsts in summer, my mother used to prepare a concoction of the roots of couch grass and liquorice sticks which were put to soak together in large coffee pots.

It was during the winter that the *fatigue du cochon* took place in many households. This was a day of intense activity. The animal was stretched out on its place of execution; a large knife plunged into its neck put an end to its final agonised squeals, and the blood was collected in a basin to form the basis of *boudin*. The pig was scalded, and its skin scraped; it was cut up, divided into bits, and the making of the pork preparations began in earnest; a machine turned by hand filled the intestines with meat in long sausage serpents; little savouries, *pâtés*, *andouillettes*, stuffed tongues, all piled up; the legs and shoulders were put aside to be turned into ham.

At mid-day, everyone involved had a taste of the animal, cooked in the oven. A special place was needed to keep all these victuals which were welcome on our table all the year round.

A big clean-up was essential after this exhausting day of activity, but it was very different from what would happen nowadays. Elbow grease was involved above anything else, to wax furniture and floors, shine the coppers, polish the stove, and beat the carpets and stairs with cane carpet beaters.

There were few cleaning products, and we often resorted to cheap and simple means; newspaper was used a great deal, as was linseed oil. Soda crystals dissolved in boiling water served for washing up, but they left a greasy deposit on our fingers and on the bowl. A lot of effort was put in without the results obtained today with the vacuum cleaner and the numerous detergents.

Thursday was washing day. As there was no school that day, I was able to see to the housework and attend to the meals while my mother did the washing.

This took place in the cellar of my parents' new house, as there was a fireplace to heat up the water and a basin for rinsing. We had the luxury of having running water; my aunt Emilie did not, and I can still see her, her heavy basket on a mat on the top of her head, hands on her hips, going to rinse her washing in the Hérault, where sometimes she would have to break the ice. I admired this spartan attitude and wondered whether I would copy her one day.

The evening before, one 'put in the soap' – that's to say, the washing was soaked in soapy water. Next day, each article was washed in the wooden or zinc tub, and the dirtiest were

34

submitted to vigorous scrubbing with a brush on a plank. A lump of washing blue was swirled around in the rinsing water; this tinged the washing slightly, and gave it a more intense whiteness.

Four times in the year, the *grande lessive* would take place. We used to gather together the large white sheets made of linen or cotton and linen, the napkins, the drying up cloths and all the large articles ... there had to be an immense stock of linen to meet all the needs of three months' use, but our cupboards were well furnished.

Once washed, the linen was piled into a large round vat, covered with a thick cloth filled with wood ash given to us by the baker, and throughout the whole day one kept the wash 'flowing' by pouring boiling water onto the ashes; the water, thus filled with potash, flowed through the washing, removing the final impurities, and ran out to the other side through a hole at the bottom of the vat. This operation made the whole place fragrant. Afterwards, all that was left to do was to load the wash onto a wheelbarrow to take it to rinse in the river, as our sinks were too narrow to move these large articles about in them. The women would kneel at the edge of the water, in front of a flat stone, and energetically shake the washing up and down in the current, then beat it with a wooden *battoir* to drive the water from the fibres.

> Tous les jours, moins le dimanche
> On entend le gai battoir
> Battre la lessive blanche
> Dans l'eau claire du lavoir.
>
> (Every day except Sunday
> One can hear the cheerful sound of the *battoir*
> Beating the white laundry
> In the clear water of the washing place)

In 1934 I taught this rhyme to my first pupils; it would have no meaning whatsoever to the children of today.

In the summer months I was allowed to go to the river with my mother. I have a glowing recollection of those mornings when I would splash about in the cool water, chasing the dragonflies, or trying to capture the small fish which darted about, and put them in a tin.

My father had a little wooden wash tub made for me, exactly like my mother's, and I used to wash my dolls' clothes in it.

For the ironing, several hot-irons were set before the wood fire or on the hot plate of the stove. One took hold of an iron with a thick handful of fabric, brought it up close to the cheek to gauge how hot it was, and then glided it over the linen, which had first been sprinkled with water.

Saint-Thibéry was subject to frequent floods: a fluctuating river, the Thongue, normally a thin trickle of water, swelled out of all proportion in heavy rain and merged with the tumbling muddy swirls of the Hérault to invade the low-lying parts of the village. I remember the floods of 1920. We had been rudely dragged from bed by the sound of the tocsin; my father went to untie the donkey, who was already in difficulties, while my mother collected linen and provisions together.

With a lantern to light us, in driving rain, sheltered by umbrellas and sacking, we set off to climb up to the Fort, which was spared from the current. Pulling a rope, my father urged the reluctant donkey to go forward, my mother got drenched trying to protect our precious goods and chattels for our exile, and for my part, I tried with as much strength as my little legs could muster to flee as quickly as possible from this shifting landscape, in which the persistent rain and howling wind were merged, and our shadows lengthened eerily on the sodden ground. At last we reached a secure haven; this was my paternal grandparents' house, situated on a road which was safe from the floods; there we met up with another part of the family who had been struck with disaster like ourselves, and for a few days I was pleased to live outside the village. My cousins and I crammed into the disused bedrooms, and the meals were different from those we had at home; my father and uncles kept us informed with a running commentary on the rising or falling of the flood waters; as they were condemned to inactivity, this was their main occupation.

Lotto, Pope Joan, Snakes and Ladders were dusted off under our fingers and stimulated lively chatter.

In the streets which were transformed into running streams,

boards were put across from one side to the other, and good balance was needed to go and replenish supplies. People even moved about in boats in some places.

When the waters receded, everyone went back home, where the *caves* smelt mouldy and some of the furniture was damaged.

Nowadays the village no longer suffers those eventualities, as a protective system consisting of powerful pumps to drive back the water has been installed.

V

During the week, I used to wear a very plain black overall, and my hair was tied back in a plait; however, Sundays were quite different: then the best clothes were taken out of the hanging cupboard; I remember one particular white dress, made for my mother's wedding trousseau, which was worn with a tulle hat decorated with elaborate flowers; my hair would be untied and I would put on the jewellery that had been given to me for my christening. I used to strike poses and make faces in front of the glass-fronted wardrobe, regarding myself with over-indulgent approval. The reason for all this pomp and ceremony was going to Sunday mass. I would take my place in church in the tiered benches near the choir, reserved for the pupils of the *école laïque*.

We sat apart from the girls who went to the convent school; they faced us on the other side of the nave. They were accompanied by two elderly ladies, secular nuns, who lived frugally, and who, in spite of their good intentions, gave an education which was greatly inferior to ours, but it was considered more 'select' to go there, amongst the children of the wealthiest families.

To help augment their slender resources, the nuns used to organise theatrical evenings which we attended, long-sufferingly: the play used to be about the martyred patron saint of our parish, Thibéry, who was tyrannised by a heathen father. I would wait impatiently for the interval, when they sold long, thin sticks of liquorice which I have never been able to find anywhere since.

The church service was an interlude of rest and gentle oblivion. I let myself be lulled by the hymns sung by the ladies in the choir, who at regular intervals would cluster and jostle round the harmonium like birds on a short branch.

The curé would go up into the pulpit; his words soared right over my head, and I only took in the sweeping play of his long sleeves. I particularly admired our doctor's daughter, who used to sit in the front row next to her mother; she had a pretty face which was set off by a beautiful fur coat, and I coveted her muff, suspended from a cord worn round her neck, in which she kept her hands warm.

Beside me sat Margot, looking a complete replica of myself as she had been told what I would be wearing ... we had at least two outfits the same.

Naturally, we celebrated our solemn First Communion together; earlier than was usual, though I don't know why; we were only nine years old.

So we were very young at the time of learning the catechism, but even so, I do remember that we were tantalised by the presence of the boys.

The week before the communion, we were allowed off school to rehearse the moves that would take place during the ceremony. We took our breaks in the courtyard of the presbytery, and, highly conscious of the faith, we invented little plays about the holy scriptures.

Before confession, we put our souls in torment to try and find a list of reasonable sins; and what relief we felt at regaining our original innocence after the penitence; we used to express it in bursts of joy.

My father was a non-believer: as a child he had been an altar boy and had been devoted to religion with all the fervour of his passionate nature; he later told me that as he grew up, he had lost his faith as the result of deep reflection. But he wanted this religious festival to be a happy memory for us. Lots of invitations were sent out to members of the family; Margot's godfather, Arthur, came from Montpellier with his wife and son; a large table was laid ready in an empty room; my mother and her sister had prepared the meal. Noelie, the pretty fiancée of Margot's eldest brother Charles, had given us the finest of her young goats for our roasting spit.

All adorned in our white finery, with coronets of camelmias (a gift from Godfather) on our heads, we were rather excited to be the centre of the festivities and we sang convincingly

Le voici l'agneau si doux
Le vrai pain des anges

(Behold the gentle lamb
Truly the bread of angels)

under the roman vaults of our church, which, on that day,
seemed transformed by our wonderment into a very cathedral.

VI

I have no happy memories of my nursery school: the school premises were ugly, the teacher was elderly, and we droned out the letters of the alphabet which she pointed out to us on the blackboard with the end of a stick. Very aware of my awkwardness, I would be close to tears when asked to draw anything, and was scarcely any better at basket weaving. Playtimes were purgatory for me: first of all, there was the terror of the cesspool, a foul-smelling pit with filthy, slippery sides, into which I was terrified of falling; then there was the school cleaner's grandson, who enjoyed the favoured position of organising the playground games; these would always consist of playing at battles; I loathed this, and found out how to avoid it; at the first enactment of an attack, I would lie down on a stone bench, representing the hospital, and would wait there without moving until it was time to go back into the classroom.

In contrast, what wonderful years I spent at primary school. In its old, rather impractical buildings, I followed the outstanding teaching ardently: Madame A, who was a bit aloof, the elegant Madame M, and Mademoiselle B, unceasingly dedicated. I owe a great deal to you, and I feel moved when I think of all you gave me.

The day would begin with our singing: 'Par milliers, venez chers écoliers' or 'Dis moi petite source', and work would begin with a lesson on morals when we would listen avidly to the teacher's advice. In the classrooms, our heavy black wooden desks with their white blobs of the inkwells, matched our blouses which were the same colour. The walls were adorned with prints illustrating various lessons, and in the elementary classroom a large blackboard stood imposingly

41

with 'Les droits de l'homme et du citoyen (the rights of man and citizen) standing out in gold letters. This made a great impression on me.

My mother used to cover my books in a cloth binding so that they were protected for the whole year long. In his beautiful handwriting, my father would inscribe the labels: 'Grammar – Marthe Boyer'. I was very proud of these possessions, and also of a decorated wooden pencil box with a sliding lid, in which I kept my rubber, my pencils and my penholder. We used to have two kinds of pen nib: the 'Sergeant Major' for general writing and the *de ronde* nib for inscribing beautiful titles on the front of the exercise book. A tin contained a damp sponge and a duster used to wipe and shine the slate, which played a big part in our studies, and the silence of the classroom would often be disturbed by the squeaking of chalks: these were kept tightly packed in their metal case.

We seldom indulged in scientific experiments, but when we did, we felt extremely proud and elevated to the rank of chemists.

A few little animals were kept: we had some silkworms which walked about in a shoe box lined with mulberry leaves, and we marvelled at their metamorphosis.

When we had exams, we used to go to school on Thursdays as well, even though that was a holiday in those days. I found these extra study days delightful: there was an unaccustomed feel to the school when there were only a few pupils in it. I often used to come second. 'Come on, Marthe,' the teacher would say to me, 'just a little more effort.' I was never able to beat Julienne. Her father owned a mechanical engineering workshop in our neighbourhood, which later became a factory. So we used to go the same rather long way home. She was a very studious girl, and would make me learn my lessons whilst walking along. This made my homework a lot easier.

I gained much satisfaction from my reports from my teachers and classmates. I used to think of my teachers as almost superhuman, and could not imagine them doing ordinary everyday tasks. It is true that in those days they did live differently from other people: living in a school, with a member of their family or a maid to take care of the house-keeping, they did not mix with the life of the village.

Later on, I kept in touch with our headmistress, Mademoiselle Bacon, and I realised what she had thought of me when I had the occasion to introduce my husband to her: 'Monsieur,' she said, 'I congratulate you on having found Marthe Boyer on your life's way.'

* * *

We had few toys when I was a child, and those were simple, but we didn't suffer because of it. The catalogues from Printemps and la Samaritaine were an inexhaustible source of cutting-out material and dreams.

We used to skip and play ball, and play at knucklebones which we polished on a wet stone and stained red in a solution of madder: we played hopscotch; a particularly chalky stone was carefully treasured to draw the squares, over which we had to hop pushing the puck, in the cobbled street which we usually used because it was nice and slippery.

On summer evenings we would play *cligné* (hide and seek) around the houses, and sometimes we used to play *le martelet*: the most impudent among us would rap on a front door, and then it was a rush to go and hide in a corner, and be thrilled when someone opened the door or appeared suddenly at a window, saying 'Who's there?', and then 'Ountes passat?' (Where's he gone to?).

Our game was innocent enough compared to the one the boys used to play at nightfall. A big stone would be suspended above the doorway of a house by a long rope which they pulled from a distance away. The sleeping person would awake with a start and utter loud expletives, to the great delight of the boys.

The jokes used to be taken a bit too far in some villages: in the middle of the *vendanges*, while the must of the precious harvest was bubbling in the *caves*, a *viticulteur* was loudly called out to in the middle of the night: 'Milou, lou bin sescampo din lo rec (Emile, the wine has all spilled into the stream). The awakened man appeared at his bedroom window, and immediately his face was smeared all over in red, with the help of a long pole topped with a cloth soaked in blood from the abattoir; simultaneously an explosion rent the air, and his terrified wife saw him stagger in with his face covered in blood...

In springtime we would bring back large bunches of poppy buds from our walks in the countryside round our houses; we used to turn these into choirboys and line them up in procession; the soft cases from the tops of reeds became whistles, and pretty flowers joined together by their stalks became necklaces and bracelets.

Hardly any equipment was needed for the usual games we knew; to play *coutelou*, for example, any little object (a coin, a marble or a pebble) would do.

The child holding the object would pretend to slip it into the tightly clasped hands of the other children in the circle. One player who stood outside the circle was called, and had to guess where the object had gone by asking, 'As lo cotelon Morron?' (Have you got the cotelon Mourrou?) To which the child who had not got it replied, 'Non Morron.' (No, Mourrou.)

Then he was asked to stand up: 'Leva-tu e cerca lo.' (Get up then and look for it.)

Then, if it was him after all, he said, 'O Morron.' (Yes, Mourrou.)

At which he was told: 'Leva-tu e fai-me un poton.' (Get up and give me a kiss.) And it would be his turn to pass on the cotelon.

We often played this Occitan game sitting in a circle in the school playground or in the street.

On Sunday we used to be given two sous to spend on sweets. Rachilde, the grocer, used to welcome our greedy expressions, and we would come away with four toffees or a liquorice cock's head. A bit later on, we had the right to a *petit pain de tortosa* which cost five sous. It stung my mouth because I ate it rather greedily all at once, while Margot savoured hers bit by bit and gave me a few extra morsels.

Sometimes the *marchand d'oublis* passed by; slung over his shoulder he carried a large red cylinder, the top part of which was a roulette wheel. For two sous he would turn the wheel which would show the winning number, and he would open up the box to give out long flaked pastry cones to us.

From time to time, on a Thursday afternoon, I would be

allowed to go to my cousins, whose house looked out over the countryside. There we would collect up the ingredients for a pretend dinner party, made up from vegetable peelings which we got from my aunt; those from the aubergines were the most prized; the round green bases made up a *gigot*, the jagged bits were cut up into *côtelettes*, and the purple skin became sausages; thus we would have a complete butcher's stall. At four o'clock we would all treat ourselves to raisin tarts covered in sliced almonds – a delicious meal made from the fruits of our own harvest.

Sometimes we would go in a group to our friend Claire; her house was huge and full of surprises. Our favourite place in it was the attic which hid a wealth of treasures: we used to dress up in costumes of bygone days, and would arrange colourful parades in her big garden, where grew an enormous fig tree and a jujube tree whose fruit we greatly appreciated. We could do anything we liked at Claire's: her mother, very busy with a large family, and full of indulgence, used to give us complete freedom. From her house we would go occasionally into a little wood nearby called Les Côtes, where we used to run wildly between the thick bushes and brought back bunches of *fragon*, the holly of the plains.

When my friends came to my home, I organised theatrical performances; sometimes I set my sights very high. Thus, one day, we performed *Deinara*, a Greek mythological play, which I had been to see in the Arènes at Béziers with my father. The characters were acted and dressed in appropriate costume, and we said our lines convincingly, perched on the platform which covered the wells, reading our parts out of the book which was passed from hand to hand. My cousin Lucille, who was tall with long blonde hair falling loose, played Hercules; Julienne, pretty and moving, draped in a large veil, was a striking Aeolus, and ... naturally, I kept the part of Deinara for myself.

VII

In those days, the young people seldom went out of the village, and the only entertainments for them to take advantage of were local ones. Couples used not to go out together. While the women went to vespers on Sundays, visited friends or busied themselves in the kitchen, the men used to go to the café to play cards. Outside their homes, families only got together for the festivals which took place in an atmosphere of great celebration: these were the carnival and the local *fête*. In between these lively periods, village life was calm, hard-working and dreary for the young.

During the carnival and the local *fête*, all work stopped; this was an opportunity to wear new clothes for the first time and to invite friends and relations from far away to enjoy the festivities and share in the gastronomic feasts.

When I was a child, the dissoluteness of carnival time used to frighten me, and I was terrified by the characters in disguise, who wore grotesque masks. I kept well away from Poulain, the mythical animal who strolled about the streets on public holidays: this was made of a frame covered with a many-coloured cloth, on which were perched two figures made of straw called Estiennou and Estienette; it was animated by men hidden inside, who shook the head of the animal at the end of a long pole which reached the upper storeys of the houses. At the street corners, men disguised in *dominos* performed the 'fig dance'; the fruit, hanging from the end of a fishing rod was offered to the children who would try and reach other end of the fishing line with open mouths.

Traditional dances followed one another throughout the day: there was the dance of the bellows, where the dancers dressed in white with red belts, nightcaps on their heads, would perform the gestures of the dance at each street crossing; with a pair of bellows in their hands, directing it at the posterior of the one in front of them, they would sing: 'Bufa li al cuol' (Blow him up his arse). Then there was the *chevalet* which mimed the shoeing of a horse and required a lot of skill. Under their arches decked with vine branches and flowers, the couples wove gracefully in and out to the sound of drums and oboes.

On the Wednesday a cavalcade made up of amusing or romantic floats processed through the village. These public events attracted many people and I used to watch the frenzied crowd from the height of my grandmother's house.

Each evening a dance was organised, and those reluctant to remove their masks suffered *lo brandol*: amid shrieks and laughter they were hoisted up and shaken until they showed their faces.

The judging of the *carnaval*, represented by a strangely dressed dummy, took place on the last day of the festivities. A full jury was set up, and the hero of the *fête* was accused of having been the cause of all the local problems – hail, unemployment, flooding etc., and even personal troubles – adultery, accidents ... he was unconditionally condemned and burnt in the village square amid the general euphoria. A circle was formed and the singing went

> Adieu paure, adieu paure carnaval,
> Tu t'en vas e ieu demori
> Adieu paure carnaval.
> (Farewell, farewell poor carnival,
> You are going and I am staying,
> Farewell poor carnival.)

Then the young people all got together to enjoy the free cakes which had been donated by public generosity.

* * *

After that, it was a long time until 14th July: this holiday was celebrated with great republican fervour in my home: the evening before we went to the open air concert given by the

Lyre Saint-Thibérienne: the pavement cafés spilled out into the square; there we would consume lemonade and beer in moderation. At one of these evenings, my mother started a panic; a very highly strung person, she was sensitive to the bombs which were going off in all directions, and in jumping up from her chair she sent the bottles and glasses flying onto the cobblestones.

The next day, our balcony used to be festooned with a beautiful tricolour flag. During the morning I was urged to take part in the sports where we could win prizes donated by the municipality. The boys took part in a game in which jugs were strung up in a horizontal line; armed with a stick and blindfold, they had to break them. Sometimes a rabbit would escape from one of them, nimbly recovered by the lucky competitor, while the less fortunate received a cold shower. Amusing sack races and egg-and-spoon races were organised too.

The mid-day meal was particularly carefully prepared that day: even though I find it barbaric to scald a living creature to death, I was delighted to find the ritual sacrifice of lobster on the table: there would also be a duck, and a variety of desserts. In the afternoon the entire population got together on the shady banks of the Hérault to join in the water sports, duck races, and balancing on the greasy pole to reach the flag at the other end.

Afterwards the dancing drew the crowds: a platform decorated with greenery was set up in the square, and this was an occasion for the elderly couples to risk joining the young ones to dance a polka or a waltz. The national *fête* didn't happen every day of the week.

* * *

The local *fête* was celebrated on the 11th of November. The village squares were filled with fairground entertainments. A timid child, I was frightened of the roundabouts, especially those which were particularly violent such as the *casseroles* and the 'big eight'. So as not to stand out, I would risk a few turns on the safe ones.

As I was greedy, I would spend most of my time in front of the sweet stalls, never tired of watching the long, multicoloured ribbon of sugar, attached to a hook, being stretched by the humbug seller.

One year, at the end of a concert, he gave my father a giant conductor's baton, made up of all the flavours from his stall.

Often stands would be set up which offered freak shows: the bearded lady, the flea trainer, the woman with three legs; this last intrigued me and I succeeded in dragging along my mother and aunt. The poor 'disabled' one was sitting on a large armchair in a sequinned costume: she made us feel her third leg: it was certainly made of flesh, but wasted away, and she lamented her sad fate. I emerged feeling very moved.

A few days later, when the fairground was packing up, what was my astonishment to see my three-legged lady, divested of her trappings, standing on two legs like everyone else. A child was beside her, and I suspected that the third leg belonged to it – I was shattered to think of the poor little thing being kept still in an uncomfortable position through the long afternoons.

The young people used to get together at the ball; chairs were set round the dance floor for the comfort of the mothers who had come to watch over their daughters; if these should be absent a little too long, there was an alert and the absconder was brought back quickly. The band played four dances in never-changing sequence: the paso doble, foxtrot, tango and waltz, and then the invitation dance, after which the young man would offer his partner something to drink.

At this stage, the café proprietors who were understanding and obliging, gave out coffee or infusions to the mothers, anxious to get them to prolong the evening.

Young girls today get onto the dance floor spontaneously: in our time one waited to be asked; it was very painful for those who weren't chosen often to *faire tapisserie*, as the saying goes.

In summer, with the benefit of warm evenings, travelling circuses would come and set themselves up on the Place du Couvent which was overlooked by my maternal grandmother's house. During the day, I would watch these ragged families, yelling at their children and horses, erecting their flimsy scenery, and my heart was touched with pity. As soon as night fell, a miracle was accomplished. They were hardly recognisable with their faces made up and their sparkling clothes. They radiated happiness. Often they would present items with highly skilled acrobats, a few pirouetting monkeys or little dogs, and they received enthusiastic applause from the grown-ups standing behind their children who sat on the benches . . . but as soon as they announced that a hat would be passed round, the crowd thinned out, and this used to disgust me.

Next day, very early, the square would be empty. A wisp of straw or some horse droppings were the only reminders of their visit, and I felt very sorry for the children, treated uncaringly, who already had to earn their living.

From Secondary School to Teacher Training College

1st movement – Allegro molto vivace

VIII

At the age of 12 I began life as a boarder at the Pézénas Ecole Primaire Supérieure for girls. We had been waiting in suspense for the competitive entrance examination until the 29th July; Juliette had been the only one to join me in this test, the five other applicants, of whom Margot was one, had been accepted to take the *examen des Bourses* in June but our headmistress had dissuaded my father from putting me in for it; in the end I came third out of 30 pupils.

The establishment was the height of discomfort and austerity: the gloomy playground surrounded by galleries had no outlook; the dormitory, with long lines of little beds divided by a central aisle, was very cold, the refectory dismal.

Discipline was strict; if we raised our voices during a meal, we were deprived of letters; silence was the rule in the bootroom and the dormitory; on the other hand we were expected to sing and dance in circles in the playground; it was forbidden to walk around in groups, particularly in pairs.

No noise was allowed in the prep room which we occupied from 7.0 to 8.0 a.m. and from 5.0 to 7.0 p.m. We had ten minutes in which to get out our books and exercise books; after that we were forbidden to open our desks: the slightest squeak of a chair or the sound of a desk being closed would be rewarded with 50 lines. So our memories were well trained with the monologues of Racine and Molière, or the Fables of La Fontaine.

On Wednesdays or Saturdays, which came before our free days, we had to work on drafting our French essays; the supervisor checked what we were doing, and sometimes picked up on untidiness, so that each phrase had to be revised several times.

We ate our breakfast in the extension of the refectory, furnished with long marble tables which had wide cracks filled with dirt; *café au lait* or black coffee was served in thick bowls or basins by means of a ladle dipped into a huge container. A single slice of dry bread was the only accompaniment to this beverage. As I did not like milk, I would drink a few mouthfuls of coffee and eat my bread, and would have gnawing pains in my stomach during the morning. The midday meal was best when we were given sausage and mashed potato; but more often, the dishes were so badly cooked that we tipped them surreptitiously into our pockets which we had previously lined with old exercise books. In this context, I remember a particular incident when a pupil from Capestang became a victim; the headmistress had caught her disposing of her portion of rice, and made her empty it out onto her plate and eat it, covered in ink blots, while threatening to lower her bursary.

Puddings used to consist (amongst other things) of nine chestnuts, some of which were rotten, or a spiced cake which we would dunk in the water to increase its volume. One day there was a big surprise on going in to lunch – we found next to our place settings an orange and a dessert. We wondered why the menu was particularly good ... but during the meal the extra goodies were taken away: they were for decoration only and we learned that the expected visit of the Inspector of Hygiene had been postponed.

Along with our school uniforms we had brought with us our cutlery and a silver mug engraved with our initials. After meals these were washed without any regard for the rules of hygiene: a basin of cold water for the mugs, and one of hot water for the cutlery were passed round from table to table; we shook our utensils about in them and then put them away in our cutlery bags ... the same water was used for all the boarders.

We spent our evenings in the corridors; to our humming of 'la la la' we would dance to warm our feet up before going to bed: dressed in a night shirt over our combinations, we would have a perfunctory wash in the washbasins which stood in rows; once a week we had a foot bath in the zinc basins. The girls who were 'indisposed' on that day could go without, because we were told that it was unwise to indulge in this washing while having a period, or to wash one's hair. On these occasions we found ourselves in a very uncomfortable predicament. The ban on going into the linen-room meant that all day long we had to carry clean underwear in our pockets ... as well as soiled.

We were paralysed by many taboos in those days. Only very occasionally did we use the town baths.

I have found my entry leaflet for the school, and this is what it said:

The Ecole Primaire Supérieure de Pézénas not only prepares its pupils for the many different examinations which open up most careers to women. Above all, it is intended to round off the education of young girls, to watch over their learning with great care, and to train them in household skills and laundry work.

Situated in excellent, hygienic surroundings, it offers every possible guarantee of health and comfort.

If the first paragraph was adhered to, the second was certainly not.

After the items which we had to take with us – all our bed linen, shoes, scarf and toilet requisites – the uniform was listed as follows:

1) One black dress
2) One jacket or coat in black cloth
3) Two white blouses (only worn after the Easter holidays)

The only trimmings allowed had to be in white or black.

When we walked in a crocodile through the town, wearing these severe uniforms, complete with black shoes and stockings (they never managed to cheer up our unimaginative uniform hat), we resembled an orphanage on the move.

That uniform hat. I knew eighteen different models in the nine years I was a boarder. None of them was very becoming, and the older we grew, the more reluctant we were to wear them. A few of the older pupils chose them, and three head sizes were allowed for.

Every Thursday and Sunday afternoon we went for a walk in the country: the route hardly ever varied from the roads to Caux or Alignan, near the school. When we were a certain distance from town, the supervisor allowed us to break ranks. At last we were able to let off steam and high spirits, and arm in arm we would sing the latest romantic songs.

Sometimes we would meet Caïffa, the pedlar who pushed an enormous container full of groceries. Then we would treat ourselves to chocolate and biscuits.

When we were told to proceed along the Castelnau road (something which very rarely happened), we hopped up and down with joy, for this meant we would cross through the town. It was a treat to be a part of the hustle and bustle of the city, which was much less apparent very early on Sunday mornings when we went to mass.

In the spring, our walks sometimes led us to la Grange des prés, the estate which is famous because of its association with Molière, who stayed several times and performed some plays there. Through the openings in the railings I would try to glimpse the large terrace of this imposing dwelling, where thespians had established themselves in the grand days of the 17th century.

I felt intoxicated with these thoughts, and this rapture was due in part to the scents of spring, dominated by the perfume of narcissi. It was not until much later that, in this very park, I attended a production of *le Bourgeois Gentilhomme* performed by the players from the Comédie Française, and my adolescent dreams came full circle.

When we walked back to school on Sunday evenings, and happened to pass a little girl with her parents, I used to feel sad, and I envied her, imagining the cosy home to which she was returning.

Margot and I seldom went out on Sundays: my mother or my aunt would take it in turns to come to the visiting room on that day 'from one train to another' as they expressed it, leaving Saint-Thibéry at eleven and going back at one o'clock. They made themselves responsible for our laundry, bringing with them our clean linen and a few provisions, and taking away what needed washing. Chocolate, nougat, cheese and salted meats replenished our food tin, and though I always had a good appetite, when it came to eating them I used to feel sickened by the rancid smell of this medley of foodstuffs. Our mothers took great care over the preparation of these extras: grilled toasts, dried figs filled with walnuts, roasted chestnuts etc., but the time spent in the wretched tin completely altered the flavours.

Sometimes we would go out in the afternoon: our mothers, simply dressed according to their taste, would take us to the *café d'un sou*. this was a gloomy chamber, in one of the little narrow streets of which there are so many in Pézénas, run by a thin woman with a pale, sad face; we drank the black liquid she served us, and ate cakes bought from the *pâtisserie* next door. We did justice to Pézénas' rightful reputation for its *berlingots* and little *pâtés*.

Some of the boarders had guardians in the town, with whom they spent the whole of Sunday: when they came back, they brought with them a breath of the outside world, and told us about the famous films of the time, such as *Sheik* which starred the handsome Valentino – something to dream about...

The world events reported in the newspapers hardly penetrated the school; in 1927, Lindberg's feat in being the first to fly single-handed across the Atlantic did not affect us; but later the kidnap of his child distressed us deeply.

The discipline was strict, and once we had gone to bed, we were forbidden to get out again before it was time to get up in the morning. During my first months as a boarder I was too worried to sleep properly, as regularly, in the middle of the night, I needed to go to the lavatory. This kept me awake, and I squirmed around in my bed, pressing my thighs together to calm my urge. Tired out by this nightly torture, I plucked up courage to tell my parents, who obtained permission for me to get up. Every night I embarked upon my dark journey. My dormitory was on the first floor and the toilets were on the second: to get there, first I had to go along a corridor cluttered with coatstands which terrified me, then go through a portion of the gallery open to the sky, and last of all I had to climb a staircase. As I needed to go, I was brave on the way there, but the way back had me trembling with fear by the time I reached my bed. Later a classmate confided in me that she had solved the problem by using a jam jar which she emptied in the morning!

I remember one night when our supervisor, aware of an unusual commotion, came in to scold us, and at our request switched on the light. What pandemonium broke out! Our bedclothes and the walls were covered in bedbugs. We did not know how we were going to get rid of them. The next day the caretaker's husband fumigated our beds with a blow-torch.

No holidays, nor any free time in that establishment: we were there to study, to work, and to win the first places in the competitive examinations. Thursday mornings were taken up with extra dictation bristling with difficult bits, and with researching locus, in which I 'dried up' miserably. In the second year (the Fifth nowadays), from eleven till noon, we had the choice between dressmaking (making a dress or a hat) or learning shorthand typing. I did the latter as I was scarcely skilled in the other subject. I had enough trouble in the sewing class learning the stitches and how to make vests, bibs etc . . .

We were not allowed to indulge in any personal adornment, and once I saw the headmistress holding an older pupil under the tap because she had curled her hair and put some light make-up on her face. For this reason, small incidents took on an exaggerated significance in our eyes.

The school possessed a library; on exchanging books, we had to hand in a summary of the one we had just read; no other publications whatsoever were allowed into the school, without serious consequences.

During the short holidays, I had taken home the book allocated to me which was *Les Oberlé* by René Bazin. I remember my father's indignation – he said we were being given vindictive books to read; his pacifism was appalled by it; and he gave me an example by citing the generous action of Aristide Briand who was in favour of reconciliation between France and Germany.

He talked to me enthusiastically of Gandhi, for whom the love of his fellow men and the renunciation of all violence came to be the guiding forces of humanity.

He would willingly have conversations with me about the social problems of which he was so aware: in particular about his outrage in 1927 at the condemnation to the electric chair of the two Italian anarchists Sacco and Vanzetti, despite their protestations of innocence. He also gave me some lessons about tolerance concerning the Dreyfus affair, which aggrieved his sense of fairness.

He sent me this card for my thirteenth birthday:

This day is just another day like all the rest, but it affirms your thirteen years and bids you to be worthy of this age, not in suppressing the delight of play or laughter, but by enabling you to achieve, in the most sensible and at the same time most honourable way, your transformation into the young girl that you will be tomorrow.

It behoved me to be worthy of such messages. I came by chance upon a letter written to my parents in 1925 (that very same year), which could not have disappointed them: 'Madame' wrote to my father: 'She is a little girl who will succeed in life.' And that is true, when I possibly can, I want to succeed, and am determined to succeed.

There were times, though, when my father would complain about the lack of care I took with my letters and about spelling mistakes: 'You know full well that these faults offend my eyes just as a wrong note offends my ears!'

Did he smile, or was he annoyed with the gem that I discovered in a letter of the 25th March 1926 when I described the joy I was feeling at the nearness of the departure for the Easter holidays: 'Le matin, quantité d'élèves allaient remuer leurs mâles (sic) en poussant des cris de joie.' (This morning, lots of the pupils went to bring out their males [malles = suit-cases], uttering joyful cries.)

I think that it is the passing of time and the attraction of life as it is today that make me judge that boarding school as harshly as I do. Though all the details are true, and there is no exaggeration whatsoever about its lack of comfort, I must admit that I was not unhappy there. My letters written at that time show that I was content, and sometimes even enthusias-tic, but it is in my nature to be lively and to emphasise the brighter side of life. Without disliking any of my classmates, I used to seek the company of those who were cheerful and who knew how to get out of essays; I steered clear of the *bucheuses* who always wondered anxiously what we had written in our compositions. I had preferential treatment from the supervisors, particularly the younger ones.

And then, there was the attraction of the lessons: we were in the hands of a remarkable team of teachers, for whom I had a real respect. I always thought highly of their teaching methods and was shocked by the criticisms which some pupils levelled at them. We were very lucky to benefit from a conscientious teaching staff and I remain very grateful for it.

Our school had an excellent reputation in the department, and we were formidable candidates in the competitive examinations.

The main subjects were of a high standard; but other subjects considered to be of less importance were fostered too. Music lessons consisted of practical study, and the theory of singing, and went on to musical dictation and part-singing in choirs. Mademoiselle Petit, who had a keen sense of music, made us listen to classical records and sometimes would play well-known pieces on the piano for us. I used to love listening to these recitals which rekindled my regret that I was not learning this instrument: my father had declared that we were not in a position to have a piano at home. To make up for it, he gave me a mandolin, on which I assuaged my passionate love of music.

The teaching of games was not really good enough. Our science teacher provided the gym lessons, I am sure against her will. She used to instruct us wearing a fur coat, with her handbag under her arm, only putting it down to show us what movements we had to make!!

So we were rather left to ourselves until the arrival of a male instructor, who was such a hard taskmaster that I would spend most of his lessons hidden in the toilets.

We had the same teacher as the boys' college for art; we called him 'Jesus' because of his beard. When we reached 15 and had some harmless relationships with his male pupils, we would use his hat as a travelling post-box; we used to slide a note under its band, and the reply came back to us by the same route. Madame B. can't have brushed her husband's headgear very often.

We were very aware of the proximity of these schoolboys

nearby, who led their lives in parallel with ours, and we used to be tantalised when we were able to meet them. On their days off lessons, the day-boys used to come and occupy the seats which lined the avenue by our school, and closely watch our windows, from which a few daring girls would wave to them in a friendly way.

One day, I too was bold in a way which still astonishes me. I was having a brief romance with a schoolboy who came from our village. During the holidays we tried to see each other more often, and reached the stage where he tried some heavy kissing, which I found very daring. We wrote one another passionate love letters, and I think we really did love each other. But, there it was, we were both boarders, and did not meet frequently. One day, returning to school from a specially granted leave of absence, I found myself alone and at liberty in the town; as this was so unusual, and succumbing to my ardour, I went to the boys' college, on the pretext of delivering a parcel – I had just bought a tart, which served the purpose ... and there we were together in the parlour, each as surprised and nervous as the other.

We were both 17 years old!

I must give credit where it is due to the memory of our headmistress, Madame Renoux, who had little care for our comfort but was very attentive to our teaching. When I was working professionally, I struck up a correspondence with her when she retired to Marseilles, and quote here from one of her letters:

It is nice to know that some of my pupils at least acknowledge the high standards that I maintained for my work, and appreciated the efforts I tried to make for the perfection of intelligence and character of the children in my charge.

Now you in your turn, are accomplishing your task with all the ardent spirit of your youth...

She was anxious about the future of her school:

My successor has changed things drastically, and it is painful for me to know that methods dear to me have been abandoned, for they were the results of deep reflection and long experience.

I am told that the number of pupils has reduced greatly. Is this true?'

She was a very able mathematician; and in spite of very short sight could keep up with the most complicated geometrical theorems. She was very enthusiastic about this subject and would exclaim:

'It's quite amazing! With just ten signs one can add up all the values.'

When I told my father of this remark, he said:

'I say that music is even better: with only seven notes one can express oneself and compose!'

What numerical and artistic magic, born of the combination of a few signs...

And so within the walls of this school, we lived out our adolescence, with its turmoils, its enthusiasms and its disappointments.

Boarding school created an artificial climate, unfavourable to the blossoming of a young girl. Our personalities were moulded in this rather rigid atmosphere, and we looked for affection which was denied us by the absence of our families. Friendship fulfilled the need for love and we exchanged passionate notes which make me smile today ... nevertheless they were important in our search for happiness.

I sometimes meet up with old girls from Pézénas; they are the ones to whom I feel most genuinely attached, and we rekindle the trust and moving recollections of our youthful years.

IX

Apart from very rare occasions, I only used to go home for the usual holiday periods.

These were joyful departures; we used to pack up our clothes in blue and white striped bags for the short holidays, and in large trunks for the long ones.

We went along the road to the station singing a song which had been made up by those who had gone before us:

Pézénas, nous te quittons
Sans regret, sans amertume,
Joyeuses, nous chantons
Notre bonne fortune
Nos malles sont finies
Baptiste* les emporte
Et la joie nous transporte
A la gare du Midi.

Un coup de sifflet
Le train se met en marche
Nous emportant vers ceux que nous aimons
Et bien souvent, dans tout ce tintamarre
Des collégiens, nous cherchons les beaux yeux etc., etc.,

(Pézénas, we leave you
Without bitterness or regret
Singing happily
Of our good fortune.
Our trunks are packed,

* Baptiste was the caretaker's husband.

63

Baptiste is bringing them,
And joy is carrying us along
To the Midi railway station.

A blow on the whistle
And the train sets off
Bearing us towards our loved ones,
And often, in all this medley
Of college pupils, we look out for
Those handsome eyes.

I was happy to take up life with my family again, to be with my parents, in my own home, and with my familiar objects around me.

In spite of my position as an only child, I was brought up quite strictly: at seven o'clock in the morning, before she went to market, my mother would come and wake me and give me a list of the household jobs to be done during the morning. Sweeping the stairs, washing the white tiles in the hearth and the sink, rubbing up the furniture and washing the floor were my daily tasks. I often needed help from my mother who would rebuke me for my feebleness.

After meals I used to clear the table and polish and put away the washing up.

Then I was allowed an hour's reading, after which I went and sat myself down next to my mother with my piece of needlework. In those days the women used to spend their afternoons sewing and knitting. Before the arrival of clothes made of synthetic material which hardly need any mending, much reparation used to be done: patches were put on the worn out places, collars and cuffs were turned etc., ... stockings and socks were knitted in cotton or woollen thread. Young girls used to prepare their trousseaux: there would be underwear in percale, of which the stitched-down seams and hems had to be finely sewn, with barely visible stitches. The school curriculum for girls included classes in which we were taught all the embroidery stitches in red thread, and besides this we all worked an alphabet in cross-stitch, first on canvas and then on a piece of cloth.

In the course of the sewing sessions that took place at home, my mother gave me the task of embroidering a firescreen in stem-stitch, and making scalloped edges to cotton squares which were then put together to make a bedcover.

Before starting the embroidery, the following had to be done:

To mark out the scallops, a tracing wheel engraved with a design was steeped in a special ink and rolled along the material to reproduce the pattern. Initials and designs were first of all traced on transparent paper and pierced with a needle. Then a fine blue powder was spread onto the paper, and escaping through the holes, it reproduced the design on the material.

All this was done in good spirits, as the work only involved the fingers, and allowed for plenty of chatter and friendly get-togethers. Thus would a housewife spend her day.

Nevertheless, I found that the 60 minutes my mother allowed me for reading were rather too short, for I adored this occupation which inspired my imagination.

Before I went to boarding school I had a subscription to *Fillette*, an illustrated weekly, which I loved. *Lisette* and *La Semaine de Suzette* were also published at that time. One day, my father, concerned for my cultural improvement, made me a member of a more educative club, as advised by *Le Progrès Civique* – an avant-garde paper which he received regularly, and *Fillette* was replaced with this periodical which I found boring ... but one did not argue with parents' decisions.

Later, when I was at home I only read those books that were chosen by my father, drawn naturally from the best authors, the reading of which was not likely to risk disturbing me...

It was the same with my musical education; under his direction I learnt ballads of the great composers and extracts from the opera ... but I much preferred the current popular songs.

One day I managed to buy myself a little book from the 'Stella' series; there was nothing erotic about the story, but it was delightfully sentimental. I revelled in it in bed at night, and hid it under the mattress during the day. My mother discovered it, and the scolding she gave me was so severe that I felt I had been totally dishonoured.

My father did not know anything about it, and I think he would have been more indulgent in only persuading me that I had nothing to gain from such reading. But I was 15, and beginning to be concerned with the mysteries of love.

When I was 11, my father had enlightened me a little already. One day I was giving him a brief résumé of a science lesson, which ended: 'The children of alcoholics are degenerate and suffer from rickets.' His attention caught, he asked me: 'Do you understand why? I'll explain it to you: it is because babies are conceived and created by the father and mother who mate together. That is why parents must be sober and in good health in order to have healthy children.'

I wondered a great deal about this 'mating', but did not dare express my curiosity aloud. I realise that my father had been advanced in talking to me about things which a child 'should not know about', but through prudishness, he did not warn me against certain standards of behaviour, and I might have been easy prey.

There was a great silence on the subject of procreation; sensuality was denounced as a shameful pursuit. Certain couples, however, defied their parents who refused to let them be together. It would be said: 'Marie and Jean are *enlevés*' (have eloped). They would leave the village for a few days with the help of friends, and then return to their respective homes – this would often end in a marriage.

* * *

We owned a small vineyard which my father cultivated with great care; it showed a very uncertain profit, however; frosts, hail, powdery mildew, mildew and drought relentlessly attacked the poor vines to diminish their yield. Then the wine-brokers would deliver the final blow by offering very low prices.

I remember my father's towering rages when the quality of his wine which had been grown on the slopes was not appreciated – the fruit of noble vines brought on to maturity with all the necessary processes, carefully watched over in his *cave* during the vinification, and improved in the huge wooden cask lined with glistening deposit.

'If you don't get out,' he would say to the broker who had

offered him a miserable price, 'I'll send you downstairs four at a time!'

The broker was a short little man who used to slip quickly away, and come back the following day with a slightly improved offer.

The *caves-cooperatives* didn't exist then; sometimes it would happen that the barrels weren't full, meaning they would have to be emptied, which risked turning the wine sour, and the merchants profited from this situation; they offered a very low price to a grower who was under pressure to get rid of this wine.

In our region, the wide plains produced large quantities of aramon wine, of low alcohol content, which was bought at the same price as wine of 12 degrees; the marketing of this aramon wine was long responsible for the deplorable reputation of our vineyards.

On 6th March 1932, my father wrote to me: 'It is depressing and discouraging that quality is thus sacrificed, whereas a careful study of the general state of the wine industry clearly points out to the growers that they should go for quality rather than quantity.'

As President of the local branch of the Confederation Générale des Vignerons, he tried to convince his fellow citizens, but he was not listened to; they were more interested in the number of hectolitres than in the content of the wine.

Half a century had to go by before his wish was granted.

* * *

I did not enjoy working in the vineyards, but in the Easter holidays I was unable to refuse: the harvest depended on it. The pale green shoots which burgeoned on the black stumps attracted pests – hairy caterpillars and cockchafers; the caterpillars were put in a tin and burnt there and then, and the cockchafers were decapitated. Sometimes I would spread fertilizer round the roots of the vines. I disliked these tasks and hated the untidy appearance of the rough country clothes. I used to grumble to my father, who went out there every day of the week in his little cart, and only came home in the evenings. He used to take a cold meal (*la saquette*) with him, and always returned with ingredients for a green country salad, delicious *repounchous*, pears, and *souquets* to feed the fire.

Sometimes my mother would follow behind him to help with gathering up the vine shoots, the manuring and treating the vines with sulphur; for this job they would leave very early in the morning before the wind got up, and it was left to me to make sure I got to school on time.

Cultivating a vineyard demanded a great deal of work of varying degrees of unpleasantness; pruning required a particular skill; afterwards the ground had to be cleared of the scattered prunings which were then laid head to tail in bundles; the fertilizer was spread in round holes (*les escourcels*) hollowed out round the roots with a mattock. A ploughman followed the horsedrawn plough and drove the ploughshare down each row to aerate the soil and destroy the weeds. When the buds appeared, they had to be protected from disease; so they were powdered with sulphur with a dusting tin, and the mildew was kept at bay by spraying with copper sulphate from a heavy spraying machine carried on one's back throughout the long days.

All these tasks are now made easier thanks to modern agricultural techniques: tractors and machines which straddle the rows spread the manure or other various treatments over large areas in the minimum of time.

* * *

If I found no charm in the vines, I was nevertheless attracted by the countryside. My father was pleased when I accompanied him on his early morning starts: these were in the lovely spring days or in summer 'just to take the air', as he would say.

The awakening of nature at dawn was a delight: all was fresh and new. The trees and bushes were full of bird song.

Whilst my father was busy working in his fields, I would stand still for a long time, contemplating the silent life in the ditches which bordered them ... the imperceptible gossamer of spiders' webs sparkling with rosy diamond drops were slung between the blades of grass which stood tall in the rays of the rising sun. These spinners of the countryside, quite unlike the nasty drab creatures we hunted out from the corners of our houses, had variegated bodies, spangled with bright spots of many colours. Nature amazed in the glistening shades of the insect world: caterpillars wore richly coloured fur coats, and the tiny creatures which crawled about in the grass each had their originality and brightness.

I used to philosophise a bit while observing them: I reflected that with one flick I could destroy all this life ... and this observation scared me.

Events have shown me that our own existence is also fragile; at the mercy of a future impossible to predict, it can stop short while at its peak...

There was one little field of vines which was my special favourite – 'le Sanpeyre', with gravelly soil, surrounded by copses and thickets, a sanctuary for rabbits. A group of almond trees bedecked in the bridal freshness of spring stood in the middle of the vines, and their fruit which my father selected at the picking (hard almonds, *amandes des dames*, *amandes noisettes*) gave a bigger return than the meagre grape harvest. I loved this wild spot, rustling with hidden life.

Through these walks in the country, motivated by making a collection of dried plants, I discovered a wide variety of wild flowers. There were the pompoms of the scabious, the clusters of vetch, the umbellifers of wild carrot, the little bells of convolvulus, the fluffy tufts of thistles, the finely chiselled points of the cornflowers, and the myriads of daisies and dandelions spangled the fields with their white and golden petals.

Apart from these discoveries, I found our surroundings monotonous: an expanse of vines as far as the eye could see.

I could see their attraction only in October, when their rich foliage turned purple and gold under the gentle autumn sky.

I must confess: I have never liked vines, perhaps because I perceive them as having made slaves of my father and my husband, for which neither of them was meant; and nevertheless I accuse myself of ingratitude for it is thanks to the profit from the vines, even when disappointing, that I had a decent life until I could start working myself.

I was always willing to go and *faire les commissions*: this was what we used to call going to buy provisions.

69

The bread was always weighed, and to make up the balance, the baker used to add a bit of *fougasse* which never reached home intact. Without my knowing it, an adventure happened to me once in this shop, which I will tell you about in verse:

> Une histoire de coing, vraiment trés véridique
> De notre boulanger, pour cadre eut la boutique
> Or donc, vous savez bien qu'en ce bon vieux temps-là
> A son four toujours chaud, on portait tous les plats.
>
> En septembre, ma mère choisit avec grand soin
> Le plus beau, le plus roux de sa cueillie de coing
> Pour que le boulanger l'entoure d'une croûte
> Pour faire mes délices, cela sans aucun doute.
> Ce jour-là, une dame d'un âge fort avancé
> Par le plus grand hasard, eut la même pensée
> Le soir venu, la commerçante avec aménité
> Nous remit nos gâteaux croustillants et dorés
> Disant: 'Notre mitron s'y est bien appliqué.'
> Le lendemain, la dame, dans sa bouche gourmande
> Eut un contact étrange; sa surprise fut grande
> De trouver sous sa croûte, un billet libellé:
> 'Marthe, je vous aime, j'ose vous l'avouer.'
> Sans prêter attention, l'aimable boulangère
> Avait remis mon coing a notre douairière.
>
> Et le tendre message fut ainsi éventé
> Et son auteur confus et bien désappointé.
> Dès ce jour, le mitron fort timide et gentil
> Lorsque j'apparaissais filait vers le fournil.
>
> Vous conter ce récit c'est bien sans vanité
> Lorsque l'on a seize ans, le succès est aisé,
> Mais depuis ce temps-là les moeurs ont bien changé
> Ce n'est plus dans les coings que l'on fait ses aveux
> Mais c'est dans d'autres coins que l'on calme ses feux.
>
> (This is a true story, about a quince
> Told by our baker and set in his shop,

70

For as you know in those good old days
To his ever ready oven we took our dishes to bake.

In September, my mother chose with great care
The most beautiful and rosy quince of her harvest
So that the baker would wrap it in a pastry crust
For a treat for me, that is certain.
That day, a very old lady
Quite by chance had the very same idea,
And when evening came, the baker's wife said kindly
As she handed us our crisp golden pies:
'Our baker's boy has worked hard on these.'
The next day, the old lady, tucking in,
Felt something odd; to her great surprise
Under the pastry was a note which read:
'Marthe, I love you, I dare to say it.'
Without paying attention, the kind woman
Had given my quince to our good old dowager.

And thus the tender message was exposed to view
And its writer confused and disappointed.
From that day, the baker's boy, so shy and sweet
Would move towards the bakehouse when I appeared.

It is not with vanity I tell this tale;
When one is sixteen, success is easy;
But since those far off days customs have changed:
No more is love protested in a quince,
But in other secret places ardent fires are quenched.)

In the grocer's, all the foodstuffs were sold in bulk. Large
jute sacks full of dried pulses, into which the children's hands
would stray, stood in rows in front of the counter cluttered
with the balance scales, the huge cheese grater, jars and a large
tin of sardines in oil which were sold individually. Cod fillets
soaked in a great basin. Almost all the goods were sold by
weight; there was no special packaging and very few tinned
goods; this state of things considerably lessened the amount of
rubbish which is so intolerable today.
There was less choice of cheese then: Roquefort, Cantal

71

(which was called *fromage de table*), Gruyère and Camembert: at home *caillé* was made by adding rennet to other milk. The little cheeses were put to strain in glazed earthenware moulds with little holes in them.

Coffee was roasted in the street, which filled with a wonderful smell.

My mother did not entrust me with buying the meat; sometimes I went with her to the butchery. The impeccable Madame Roques (how did she manage to keep her overall so white?) presided behind a meticulously clean counter. It always surprised me how many little weights she put in the pan of the scales, which made me say mischievously to my mother: 'With all your little weights you could buy Pesquié' (one of the best wine properties in the village).

Our open air market was lively: gardeners lined up their baskets, full of their produce, and there were itinerant stall holders, but the undisputed queen of the market was Mathilde, the fishwife, with her high and mighty voice and her haughty appearance. If a competitor turned up, he was swiftly told where to go.

We were given information about the market and the life in the village by the *précon*. He had been wounded in the war, and wore a jacket from which hung an empty sleeve. He used to proceed through the streets, always stopping at the same crossroads, and having blown his trumpet, would make his announcements in a loud voice.

'Avis à la population!' preceded all his proclamations, time and time again.

Each evening the woman who sold shell-fish walked up and down the village, crying 'Aux moules frais!'

One day, on my way home from shopping, I met the flat wagon pulled by the mournful donkey of a market gardener, who daily sold her produce in the village; I bought a melon, the scent of which had tempted me. When I got home, I was scolded for buying something without having been asked to do so.

There used to be crafts in the village in those days, which have either practically disappeared now, or have changed.

The blacksmith used to work his enormous bellows to blow up the fire; a burst of sparks sprang from the glowing metal which he shaped with his hammer. When he shod the horses, a smell of burnt horn filled the surrounding air, and I used to inhale it with pleasure when I went to see my cousin Fernand who plied this trade. There was quite a ceremony to the process: the horse was tied up to a strong ring on the wall of the forge; its owner patted it with his hand while supporting its foot in a strap which he held under his arm. The blacksmith took off the worn shoe and filed down the horn of the hoof onto which he applied the red-hot metal: an acrid smoke rose up.

This procedure was watched with interest by the regulars, and in bad weather the *vignerons* who were not working would add to their number.

The cartwright made and repaired wooden yokes and shafts, much used in those days: the cooper skilfully put together the pieces of wood to make barrels. The saddler had several functions: he repaired harness and saddlery, he padded seats, with his mouth full of studs so as to have them at hand, and with the to and fro motion of his machine bristling with curved teeth, he carded the wool for mattresses.

The cobbler in his shop used to slap the soles on his leather apron; I remember going to ask him for some pitch tar to cure an infection which had arisen because of a thorn in my finger.

The embroiderers wore out their eyes doing the finest of sewing. The ironers' workshops hummed like a beehive with their female workers goffering bonnets, starching curtains and stiff shirt collars with the *fer à glacé*, and flouncing dresses; the numerous irons were heated on the many sides of an octagonal charcoal stove.

Humbler, but hard-worked, were the *bugadières*, hired for the big laundry wash.

Milk was distributed to the door by the *laitières* who owned cows and goats; they went through the village streets with their pitcher and measure and we waited on the doorstep for them to come by.

There were also itinerant tradesmen, such as the rabbit skin collector (*lo pelharoc*), who roused the streets with the cry: 'Pel de lebre, pel de lapin' (hare skin, rabbit skin). The children clung terrified to their mothers' skirts, for they used to be threatened that if they misbehaved they would be put into the sacks of these unpleasant-looking men. On certain days, the cry of Germaine the umbrella mender rang through the streets; with umbrellas clutched under her arm, she would sing: 'On raccomode les parapluies, la faïence et la porcelaine' (I mend umbrellas, earthenware and porcelain).

Though these picturesque trades have disappeared now, we have witnessed great developments which have transformed and improved our everyday lives.

Electricity, for example; what a magic fairy it is, giving us light at the simple touch of a button; our first light bulbs were topped with little hats made of opaline with frilly edges.

Gas was introduced into all houses once it had been put into portable containers: this was a new convenience for the kitchen, clean and adjustable, with quick results.

We have witnessed the birth of the sound film, and then the talkies. Things which are taken completely for granted today, aroused our astonishment and awe.

For women conscious of their appearance, the permanent wave was a precious discovery: the first attempts were achieved with wires descending from the ceiling with clips on the end which held onto the hair.

Then came the development and popularisation of the motor car which made travelling easier.

X

Sundays were spoiled by vespers during the holidays: the first mass of the day was pleasant enough, in a bright church, filled with light: but vespers under dark vaults, where we chanted gloomy canticles, were followed by never-ending telling of the rosary for a desperate length of time. Margot and I used to try and slip out before the end, but the watchful eyes of our mothers froze us to the spot. We would make the most of our regained freedom to go and watch the train pass by: this pretext allowed us a stroll with our friends along a lovely shady road, with little traffic on it in those days. There we would pass a group of boys of our own age, who had gone there with the secret intention of meeting us: we hoped for the same, but when the time came, we didn't dare approach them.

We really were ridiculous!

The Easter holidays used to be overshadowed by the religious services. We went often to church, even on the evening when missionaries came to preach the Holy Word with passion; they were very indiscreet during the confession, and this used to make me ill at ease... My tolerant father was always punctual at the evening meal to make it easy for us to go to these services which were so important to my mother. I often used to doze off with the smell of melting wax and incense. I loathed the ritual of Good Friday: this interminable ceremony ended when all the candles finally guttered out, and I would watch their slow burning with great impatience; the singing which accompanied it was monotonous and doleful.

I have been pleased to discover that Princess Palatine expressed some similar feelings in her letters. This is what she wrote on 14th April 1798:

'I have emerged from the gloom where they have been

singing from four o'clock until half past six. It is surely the most melancholy sound that one could listen to.'

Thank goodness, there was the Easter Monday party: with our mothers' help, we prepared cream desserts and cakes: making tradition an excuse on this occasion, we dared to invite the boys to come and join us. The banks of the Hérault made a fine place to have our feast, play games and indulge in some innocent embraces.

At Pentecost, when I came home, I was overcome with the freshness and abundance of the garden, which my father tended so well; it was tempting to pick everything in the vegetable garden. The spirea curved its white clusters on the wells, the trellis was bursting with roses: it felt really festive. I let myself be taken over by this exuberance of nature ... and I feel this enthusiasm still – this taste for life – and I rejoice in it.

My pleasure during the long holidays was even greater: two long months without school work! Oh, the splendour of summer when it was hot, the days were long, our clothes were light, and the shining certitude was – we were going to the sea!

We used to go to the beach every Sunday. Saturday was taken up with making everything ready. My mother busied herself with the meals, which had to be plentiful; my father attached a table and the folding chairs to the underside of the cart, and loaded up the canvas and the pegs for the tent.

The next day we were off at 6 a.m.; I used to jump nimbly out of bed; Margot and I took our places on the coupling, with our backs to my mother and father who sat in front. On the way we would meet other vehicles and call out happily to one another. My cousin Fernand followed us on a bicycle; my father set store by his presence as he was skilled at putting up the tent; we girls used to be a bit frightened of him as he used to make us swallow huge mouthfuls of sea water.

On the way, we would stop at our usual place to eat our breakfast, by the railings of les Comtesses, a private property. The drive through Agde along the banks of the Hérault was delightful; my mother never failed to buy some of the renowned meat *pâtés* to begin our mid-day meal. From time to time, at our request, my father agreed to make a halt at l'Agenouillade; a statue of the Virgin stands there, facing the sea, where, the legend goes, she stilled the angry waves by kneeling down in front of them.

Many visitors went to worship in the little chapel there: but what attracted Margot and me was the prospect of buying *taraillettes*, toys in rough clay pottery: there were plates, casseroles, jugs, candlesticks, and most important of all, the *rossignols*, little hollow birds that one filled with water and blew into to imitate a singing bird.

On arriving at the beach, we had the immense stretch of fine sand all to ourselves at this early hour: we used to feel intoxicated with the scent of iodine, the intense blue of the sea which came to lap round our bare feet ... and we spent a long day in front of this infinite horizon, our bodies feeling alternately the chill of the water and the heat of the sand.

One morning we watched some drag net fishing in progress: two groups of men and women, quite far apart on the beach, pulled a rope in a curve while approaching each other gradually. At last they met up, and the huge net pouch was drawn up on the sand. Brilliant sheens teemed in the hoop net in which a multitude of varied fish were jumping about.

That day the fishing had been good, and the fishermen's efforts rewarded.

I remember how decorous our costumes were. My father used to wear a blue and white striped bathing suit which came down to his knees. My mother's modesty was such that her scruples actually let her down; thinking it too daring to wear a bathing costume, she bathed in an old frock which billowed up in the water making her more indecent still. As for us two, our mothers had made navy blue bathing suits with white spots, not too low in the neck, and without sleeves, and we pushed our hair into mobcaps made of oilcloth which were not very becoming.

All the women wore big, wide-brimmed hats, and some of them even used parasols, for the skin had to be protected from the effects of the sun, and a pale complexion preserved.

What with collecting shells, fishing for *tellines*, and washing up at the water's edge, all was play and happiness for us, and in the evening we would return home to the slow rhythm of our vehicle, drunk with fatigue and pleasure. As our seats faced towards the back, my parents attached us to the bench with a strap, as we were likely to fall asleep during the journey! This was our first seat-belt.

* * *

September, or sometimes the end of August was the time of the *vendanges*; one sensed its approach some time beforehand: the *comportes* were put out to dry in front of the doors, the air resounded with the sound of hammers striking on the cask, the *caves* were washed down with copious amounts of water which revealed their pot-bellied vats and their wine-presses ready for action.

One morning, very early, what commotion! The work force stands around the cart which is loaded up with stacked *comportes* and poles; everyone takes a part in this loading up, and the vehicle sets off amid a happy tumult and a clanking of metal, rattling along the ruts of the vineyard paths. The journey is constantly enlivened with cries and curses, the whinnying of horses, and encounters which provoke greetings and loud questions: we are off to gather the fruit of a whole year's labour: the weather is going to be lovely we feel sure. Once we reach the vines, the cart is emptied; the men help the women down, the children jump off nimbly, and the baskets of provisions and the *bouteillous* containing fresh water are put in a sheltered place under the dense foliage of a strong vine. We get ourselves ready: on goes the strong canvas apron, the straw hat, or scarf knotted around the head, and with a basket over the arm, secateurs or cutter in hand, off we go towards the line of vines.

While we are getting ready, the men are putting the *comportes* down at equal distance apart in the *passages* (the paths) spaced about every eight or ten rows according to the number of pickers. Work begins! The rhythm is fast to start with, and one can hear the click of the secateurs cutting off the heavy bunches to fill the bucket which one empties into the *comporte* with the *quicheur* standing alongside: with his heavy, sticky hammer he crushes the grapes and protests if any leaves are mixed in. The work proceeds at a good pace until we pause for a hasty breakfast – with a good appetite. Thanks to mutual help, everyone reaches the end of the row at the same time. Jokes burst out, village anecdotes (often scandalous) are spread around complacently, and from time to time a story is intoned and taken up in unison. Sometimes the *patron* becomes angry: lifting the branches of a vine he notices some grapes at the bottom: 'This is what makes the wine; they must be picked!' But the jokers who carry the full *comportes* to the edge of the road by slipping their poles under the handles are thrilled when a girl has forgotten to pick a bunch: it's an excuse for a *capounade*. After a chase among the vines, the fugitive is captured in strong arms, smeared with the sweet sticky juice, and given a hug and a kiss despite her efforts to free herself. She will take her revenge with the help of some of the women, by stuffing vine leaves down the shirt and trousers of the young man. The driver of the wagon tries to speed things up so that he can make his journey earlier – that is, when he has a complement of 10 to 12 full *comportes*.

When the *comportes* are lined up on the road, the porters set to with combined energy and heave them up onto the cart which takes them to the *cave*. The inhabitants of each village used to increase their team with those from neighbouring villages, who had a particular nickname which was inspired by some attribute or local significance. When two work forces from neighbouring villages met up they shouted at each other in an unfriendly way; thus the people from Florensac whose vines were mixed up with ours would call us 'Baisa barrolh' (lock-kisser) and we responded by making fun of them with 'Bada moscas' (bad flies): an old legend related that in the year 391, the governor of the city of Agde had a son, Thibéry, who under the influence of his private tutor, Modeste, became a Christian, provoking the wrath of his father who drove him from his house. Thibéry, with Modeste, embarked on a frail boat and travelled up the course of the Hérault which led him to Cessaro (the ancient name of Saint-Thibéry). Thibéry possessed remarkable gifts of healing; simply by his touch, he cured people suffering from incurable diseases and his fame spread for miles around. The pagans became alarmed at this renown and beheaded him; he was buried on the spot and later a chapel was built on the site. A supernatural power was attributed to his remains, and in the town archives are details of the visit of Charles VI, King of France on the 20th November 1389 ... the town, thus called Saint-Thibéry in memory of the martyr, became a place of pilgrimage. People who were insane were shut up in the tower opposite the church, and only came out to go to the religious services. Getting them back again was often difficult; certain unfortunates resisted and would grab hold of the huge outside lock with all their might; they would bite into it, and this desperate gesture was called 'kissing the lock'. This lock still exists today, and it is claimed that kissing it prevents madness. This miraculous virtue is derided with scorn in the surrounding villages, and when someone exhibits wild behaviour it is said with irony: 'lo caldrà menar a Sant-Thibéry per li faire baisar lo barrolh' (he must be taken to Saint-Thibéry to make him kiss the lock!)

At mid-day we look for a shady spot to have something to eat: the food tins come out of the baskets; sometimes the cold meal is replaced by sausage or cutlets grilled on the spot; if a lot of snails have been found, a *fouirade* is made: the creatures are placed shell side down on the earth, covered with straw and dried grass which is set alight, and they are savoured afterwards with just a sprinkling of salt. After the meal we lie down on the bare ground for a short nap.

During this time the children play on a swing made by placing one *comporte* so that it balances between two others.

The *meneuse* gives the signal to get back to work; it is hard to bend down while one is digesting one's food, and the sun beats down strongly ... from time to time we straighten up to ease stiff backs and make the most of a gentle breeze. With what pleasure we see the carter coming back bearing a carboy of fresh water with the empty equipment which will be filled up again by the end of the day; impatiently I wait for the signal to let up, for I never enjoyed this work. I used to sigh in front of an abundantly fruitful vine, and could not understand the enthusiasm of the adults who exclaimed, 'What a beautiful vine! I am going to enjoy myself: it will fill my bucket.' I preferred the puny plants from which I picked two or three bunches without putting my bucket down, and I would be delighted when I had the chance to happen on a *dimanche* – a young stock which had not yet borne fruit.

The heat was unbearable, we sweated, the clothes stuck to our skin, we were filthy... so with what keenness I would get myself tidied up and attractively dressed as soon as I got home, and I was happy to go and shop for provisions.

The village took on a new interest, and had an unaccustomed feel; the shops were taken by storm; the smell of fermenting wine came from the *caves* and floated in the air; the streets were very lively: the *garachs* (people from the mountains) who had come to hire themselves out as workers, wandered about with their heavy gait and extraordinary get-up. Then I used to go and have a look at the dance hall where people danced every evening to the sound of a mechanical piano. A little incident happened to me there: I couldn't resist wanting to go and dance (which I was not allowed to do) and while I was twirling round, either a cat or a dog also enjoyed itself eating up the sausage my mother had asked me to get; only the wrapping remained on the bench where I had put it. I don't remember how the story ended, but certainly very badly, otherwise I would not have forgotten.

The working day was not over for my parents: my mother had to prepare the evening meal and the *saquette* for the next day. As for my father, the *cave* often kept him busy until midnight.

In those days, each winegrower made his own wine: he crushed the grapes in the *fouloir* by dancing on the bunches with his bare feet; the juice flowed on into the cement vats by means of pumps worked by hand. With the pressed bunches of grapes put to ferment for a few days in the tuns, the *pressurée* was set up; the grapes were spread onto the wine press in a compact pile; then they were compressed by tightening the screw with a backward and forward movement of a horizontal iron bar. The expressed juice flowed into the *tempot*, a little vat which was hollowed out in the floor. How many evenings during the *vendanges* I spent pushing that iron bar with my father!

'Come on, Marthe,' he would say to me, 'courage, just another little push.' I found it hard; I was dropping with sleep, and I cursed the vines yet again.

I was pleased when my cousins came to lend a strong hand; for a start that changed my father's mood, which was very tense during the *vendanges*, and my mother would prepare a *bouillabaisse* for her nephews' enjoyment that evening.

I could understand my father's anxiety, for there was always the fear of bad weather which could wreck the harvest at the last moment. 'Until the wine is in the vat,' he used to say, 'one is not at peace.'

We were among two or three winegrowers who combined forces for the picking, and when the weather was changeable, we had to wait our turn and accept the risks.

Nevertheless, on rainy days, we put on our work clothes so that we were ready to go out at the sign of the slightest clear patch ... and it was hesitations and contradictory orders that would aggravate tension in the atmosphere.

Between showers we would set off bravely along the road to the vines, and most often we came back completely soaked having scarcely got any further with the picking.

On the last day of the *vendanges*, all the work force made the most of the *sarde*, a country feast given by the owners of the vineyards: huge rounds of sausage and grilled cutlets were preceded by *charcuterie* and followed by cheeses and desserts. This meal took place amid general good spirits. The cart was decorated, the horse decked out with vine branches, and the procession into the village was as exuberant as the generous quantities of white wine.

I started harvesting the grapes when I was nine years old: two of us 'led the row', who were, of course, Margot and myself. That year the work force was made up with gypsies, often laden down with babies who spent their day under a vine, or hanging from their mothers' breasts. My heart was wrung with compassion and I felt a real sense of distress.

After that, the Marseillais or Aveyronnais came to help us: their ways and dialect, different from our own, introduced a novel and amusing note into our group.

Then the Spaniards, who arrived in their hordes, attracted by the wages, formed the largest contingent of *vendangeurs*; but this temporary immigration dwindled after the mechanisation of the harvest and the improvement of the Spanish economy after Franco.

With the end of the *vendanges*, autumn came to the country-side with its palette of glowing colours and the gentleness of its sky; the winegrowers could take a break until the leaves fell; some of them spent their time hunting in our sweet-smelling *garrigues*, others did odd jobs in their *caves* and the idle ones clustered round the Croix de la Mission, a sort of forum, to converse and often make fun of the passers-by.

XI

Autumn, for me, signalled the start of the school year, which began on the first of October. In 1930, this meant a change in my life and separation from my beloved Margot. I was going to the Ecole Normale in Montpellier. I had been turned down the previous year, but the disappointment of my failure had been alleviated by troubles concerned with the running of the competitive examination. As the pupils of a certain establishment had had knowledge of the papers in advance, the exam had to be sat again, to the great annoyance of my father, as this doubled the cost of staying at the hotel. *'Un examen saboté'* was the huge headline in the local newspapers.

Apart from the leaving certificate at Pézénas, which I passed with ease, we had to go to Montpellier for the written exam. I did not complain about it as we didn't travel much in those days and the journey by train seemed like an expedition to me. I looked out eagerly from the door of the train, ready to discover new things. Seeing an expanse of broom made me declaim:

> Les genêts doucement balancés par la brise
> Sur le vaste plateau font une houle d'or
> (The broom gently swaying in the breeze
> Makes a golden swell on the vast plain)

I was stopped short by my father who judged this behaviour not seemly nor according respect for the position of an examination candidate.

The bustle of the station, the broad avenues and beautiful buildings of Montpellier astonished me, but it was the stay at the hotel that most impressed me! I marvelled at the comfort of the rooms and was a little intimidated by the service. We did not stay up late in the evenings, which were very hot, but the short periods that we spent on the terrace of the Café Riche filled me with pride.

My father had two candidates in his charge, his daughter and his niece, Margot, whose lives had always run parallel to each other. Alas! This examination made their paths diverge for a while.

When, in the anxious silence of the whole assembly awaiting the announcement of the results, my name was read out first by the Head of the Ecole Normale, my father embraced and hugged me tightly; this was his only reward. Margot's name was on the subsidiary list; our return was sad, and the family welcome unenthusiastic; Margot's success had been hoped for more than mine; I was an only daughter, and affluent it seemed.

Thus, on 30th September 1930, my cousin and I went in different directions for the first time, but both in search of the same goal. In those days, young girls who wanted to become employed by the state had only two possible openings: the Post Office and teaching, the latter being reserved generally for the brightest pupils.

Margot went to prepare for the *Brevet supérieur* at the Ecole Primaire Supérieure in Béziers, while I became trained as a teacher at the Ecole Normale.

What delighted me most on the day of my entry into the establishment was to meet up again with Lucette, who was a very dear friend of mine. To be honest I hardly gave a thought to the security of my future, nor the future happiness of teaching.

I found this school very different from the one I had just left, with its parlour which had a polished parquet floor, its grounds which did not resemble a school playground, and its trees which were not the usual plane trees. The dormitories on the first floor consisted of a series of cubicles divided off by curtains; this gave us a certain privacy; we each had our own dressing table with wash bowl and jug.

What thrilled me most was the freedom we enjoyed; this was intoxicating after the severe discipline at Pézénas. In the large prep room which was used together by all three years, we maintained our supervision by ourselves. Aline, who was my namesake, and I would sometimes break the silence; our working together led to some misbehaviour; we would be told '*Les Boyers soeurs à la porte*' (Out you go, Boyer sisters). As we were good girls, we obeyed and we would go and continue our noisy studies outside; the room looked out over a terrace which was called 'the real world', for from there we could see the activity in the street which ran alongside the school; if we went down a few steps we would find ourselves in a field, a great expanse of wild grasses where a rudimentary tennis court was laid out, and a covered yard where the gym equipment was kept. All round about was a series of little gardens which were cultivated by the pupils; some of them were a riot of flowers; mine was very poor, as I was not very keen on agricultural tasks. In my free time I preferred to listen to extracts from *The Barber of Seville* and *In the Steppes of Central Asia*, for which I borrowed the school gramophone and took it into the meadow; lying down in the grass, with nothing but blue sky around me, it gave me the illusion of escaping into the countryside. I have to admit that I was rather unmotivated to academic study. I had worked so hard for the exam that I longed for a bit of relaxation. The exam syllabus was very full, and we cluttered up our minds with a mass of historical, geographic and scientific knowledge which I found very tedious. In spite of my poor enthusiasm for certain subjects, I was outstandingly successful in the three exams for the *Brevet supérieur*. I always had better exam results than I deserved. If certain other students lost their nerve, I was completely laid back. I would say to myself: 'Well, here we are! Here's an end to the cramming!' and I just put all my effort into it.

We had both sexes in our team of teachers, and I used to prefer the male members of staff.

Monsieur B. made mathematics attractive by the clarity of his explanations; as for Monsieur P., he enlivened his history and geography lectures with a delicate wit.

I was very disappointed to learn that the only modern foreign language taught was Spanish. Thanks to the excellent teachers in Pézénas, I had reached a commendable standard in

English, and would have liked to continue with it. So I was not very keen to make an effort to learn Spanish! The teacher who ran the class was a tacit accomplice. My position as first in my year had elevated me to the rank of librarian, and the teacher, whose daughter was studying for an arts degree, asked me to obtain extracts from various works which would help her daughter's thesis, the text of which she confided to me. I took advantage of this research to get out of numerous lessons. I made a big mistake to be proud of this, for these gaps have served me badly in my professional life, where I have often had dealings with Spanish emigrés.

The headmistress used to give us a weekly *causerie*, when she would talk to us about current affairs in France and the rest of the world: thus in 1932, we heard of the feat of Costes and Bellontes' flight from Paris to New York, an event which held promise for bringing people together and hope for future fraternity.

More dramatic was the assassination of Paul Doumer, President of France, by the Russian Gorguloff. People started to talk about a certain Hitler, Chancellor of the German Reich, but without great anxiety.

We never suspected the terrible tragedy which this man would unleash in the world, and his mad dream of exterminating whole nations...

The music lessons were very disappointing. Many of my classmates dreaded the musical dictation, and as this came easily to me, I used to place myself where the others could crib from me. We did, however, learn some pretty songs with which we began and ended the day. Madame S. used to tell us 'It's your morning and evening prayer.' The school where we did the apprenticeship for our future profession adjoined the Ecole Normale. The infant school was run by Mademoiselle V. informally called Mireille. We both liked and feared her. She had an unprepossessing appearance, but her love of children and her highly professional conscientiousness earned her the respect and admiration of all the student teachers. She tried to convert us to her methods and to inspire us with her beliefs, and she was really distressed when she failed. She gave me a little book, full of her principles – among others, 'Fais bien ce que tu fais! (What you do, do well). This made me exacting in my work. Mademoiselle F. was in charge of the primary school; I found her colourless compared to the strong personality of Mireille. The school was in a deprived area, and Mademoiselle F. must have had many occasions to show her great generosity and her love for the poor.

Periods spent working at the next door school constituted an essential part of our teaching practice:

In the first year, we were observers, attending classes taken by our older fellow students. In the second year, we had to conduct one lesson per week, and by the time we reached the end of our training we had to provide a regular week of lessons in each section.

Each week we had to make a presentation of a model lesson; we used to prepare it in groups, and one student who was chosen by drawing lots, had to present it to the children concerned in the presence of the headmistress, the teachers, and the children's form mistress. All this performance made a great impression on us.

I still had my imaginative, frivolous temperament, and was surrounded with carefree, hpppy-go-lucky friends: eight of us formed a band called the 'A.U.E.s'; I don't know where the choice of the three initials which made up our rallying call came from – they were not very remarkable, it's true. Perhaps it was a reminder of the discordant hooting of the motor cars as they drove about on the avenues of Montpellier in the 30s. We used to have joint celebrations of our *fêtes* and birthdays, and give each person a present of something they would like. For my 19th birthday, my gift overwhelmed me. My friends had made me a crystal wireless (the first sort of wireless telegraphy), with which I could receive the Montpellier broadcasting station. What wonderful evenings I spent in my cubicle, headphones over my ears, all alone with my passion for music!

There were many special celebrations which took place in the college, organised by each year in turn.

The 'first-years' were given a welcoming party, to which they responded with a 'thank-you' party.

At Christmas, the 'second-years' used to put on a living *tableau* in the dining hall. Ours depicted the angels appearing to the shepherds. Maryse, looking ethereal in her long white robe, with a premonition that her end was near, wanted to have the part of the angel; she left us only a few months later.

La fête de la déscente marked our halfway stage in the establishment. We took a few liberties and sometimes made up songs, about the college staff:

I avia una directriz
Que fasia que sospira
Ai tralalera, ai tralalala.
I avia una economa
Tojorn seguida de sos gats
Ai trulalalero, ai trulalala.

(We have a headmistress who does nothing but sigh;
We have a bursar whose cats follow her everywhere.)

We also expressed how fed up we were with our uniform hats to the tune of *'Les gars de la marine'*:

Refrain:
Voici les chapeaux d'uniforme
Tantôt jaunes, tantôt bleus
Ils sont toujours merveilleux
Ils sont variés dans la forme
Du p'tit jusqu'au plus grand
Toujours une boucle sur le devant
Quand on défile sur l'Esplanade
On entend des propos plaisants;
'Regardez donc l'Ecole Normale
A chaque début de saison
C'est toujours elle qui donne le ton.'

Couplet 1
Ils sont délicieux, on ne trouve pas mieux
Même les plus coquettes trouvent le choix heureux
C'est nous qui choisissons, après que la Direction
A déjà décidé comment elle veut nous coiffer.

Couplet 2
Mais pour les conserver longtemps frais et coquets

On préfère les quitter au coin de Boutonnet
Ne vous étonnez pas; le dimanche sur l'Espla
Si vous ne trouvez pas ces beaux uniformes là.

Dernier refrain
A baso les chapeaux d'uniforme
Qui nous coûtent quarante francs
Et ne valent pas l'argent
A bas les chapeaux d'uniforme
Qu'ils soient ronds, qu'ils soient pointus
Les Normaliennes n'en veulent plus.

(*Chorus*:
Here come the uniform hats
Sometimes yellow, sometimes blue
They are always wonderful
And of different shapes and sizes
From the smallest to the largest
And always with a loop on the front.
When we walk in line along the Esplanade
We hear pleasant comments:
'Look at the Ecole Normale
It's always they who set the tone
At the beginning of each season.'

1st verse
They are delightful, nothing could be better,
Even the most elegant find them a happy choice
It is we who choose them (after the headmistress
Has already decided what she wants us to wear).

2nd verse
But to preserve their charm and freshness for a long time
We prefer to leave them at the 'Boutonnet'
Don't be surprised if on Sunday on the Espla
You do not see these beautiful uniforms.

Last Chorus
Down with the uniform hats
Which cost us forty francs

And aren't worth the money
Down with uniform hats
Whether they're round, whether they're pointed
The Normaliennes don't want them!)

In October 1934, the new headmistress, Madame Collet, marked her entry into the college by abolishing the uniform hat... My year did not benefit from this liberal step.

At the end of the scholastic year, families and friends were invited to the *fête de l'Amicale* which took place in the open air. That day we welcomed past pupils, who shared our meal (greatly improved for the occasion). We used to make fun of their tender feelings at returning to the setting of their adolescence, and of their enthusiasm in doing so, never suspecting that we would feel exactly the same later on.

I loved the celebratory displays, and was thrilled to take part in them; I sang, danced in ballets, and acted: *Le duo des deux meunières*, in which Jeanine dominated me with her pure voice, Musset's *A quoi rêvent les jeunes filles*, and Dickens' *Cricket on the Hearth*, which aroused the demon in me which was already smouldering there.

In 1931, my first year at the college, we celebrated the 50th anniversary of the non-denominational state school system with combined displays on the big Place du Perou in Montpellier. At the rehearsals we were alongside the boys from the Normale and this put us into a fluster. We used to call them *les pingouins*, as a reminder of the black frock coats and white shirt fronts which they were made to wear in the past; now their dress was formal but unceremonial. Some of our parents tried to influence us, telling us that we would find our future spouses in this educational breeding ground; some of my classmates did indeed find charming husbands there; but I did not respond to some no doubt sincere approaches from these colleagues.

This special celebratory year ended with a pleasant surprise: we had been invited to spend four days in Paris on the occasion of the international colonial exhibition, for the modest sum of a hundred francs, the exhibition society and the Government funding our entrance fee and the cost of our stay.

My parents subscribed to this initiative, all the more enthusiastically when my father realised there was to be a music
festival on in the Paris area. This expedition was for both boys
and girls, and would take place in the long holidays. With my
case excitedly packed, suddenly a telegram arrived from
Montpellier two days before our departure: 'Marthe's journey
cancelled. Lack of parents' permission.' In spite of my father's
denial that the accompanying escort had anything to do with
it ... I was left on the platform feeling very bitter... It wasn't
until 1962 that I visited Paris.

We used to take a cheap day excursion at the end of the
school year – nowhere very far away: in the first year to
Nîmes, Avignon in the second year, and to Arles in the third
year.

Message, the Ecole Normale's news magazine, now tells of
trips to England, Egypt or Greece... I believe that we used to
have the same enthusiasm and joy at escaping, even for a
short time, from our familiar surroundings. We used to be
accompanied by a teacher and the headmistress of the next
door school; our meal, at a restaurant, was a festive occasion,
and we would enliven it with singing songs; Monsieur Puech,
who was our guide in Nîmes, was charmed by my rendering
of Massenet's *Pensées d'automne*.

Thursday was the day we were allowed to go into town to
visit the dentist: it is surprising that Madame was not very
concerned by the state of her boarders' teeth!

I had cousins living in Montpellier who became my guardians. I used to love going to lunch with them on Sundays, as
the atmosphere was very friendly; we used to go to the cinema
in the afternoon, quite often to the Salle du Capitole; a seat
cost nine francs. It was there that I saw the first talking films,
which had in fact, been in existence since 1927. These sessions
made me very keen on the film stars of the time – Gaby
Morlay, Victor Francen, Anabella etc., and Henri Garat, whose
photo adorned the underside of my desk top. Once a month
we enjoyed a long Sunday exeat from 8.00 a.m. to 8.00 p.m.

From my second year, I spent this long day off at Frontignan
in the home of Lucette, who was newly married; there I found
myself in a cosy environment with a treasured friendship;;
depending on the season, we used to stroll in the *garrigues* or

made the most of the beach, bringing back either a wealth of sweet-smelling plants, or different sorts of shells.

For these outings I exchanged my school hat for more attractive headgear, and wore more unorthodox clothes, often made by myself, for thanks to the help of some skilled classmates, I had made great progress in sewing and knitting. Woollen pullovers were in fashion, and we learned how to do more and more complicated stitches and original designs.

One night a ludicrous event took place. We awoke with a start to the crash of glass and incoherent shouts; a light flashed on in the dormitory, and sitting up, terrified in my bed, I found myself surrounded by three grinning fellows – I leapt out of my cubicle and ran to take refuge in the supervisor's room, already occupied by my terrified companions; we made alarming suppositions about this invasion, so much so that we made ourselves cry out in terror, and a great commotion ensued! We managed to restrain Maryse who wanted to jump from the second floor, crying hysterically 'I don't want those boys to touch me.' Those 'boys'? Perhaps escapees from Font d'Aurelle, the mental asylum near our college? We trembled like leaves until our supervisor came to reassure us, telling us that they were some students who were finishing their 'rag' procession in a rather impertinent manner! This intrusion resulted in scenes which greatly delighted the young men: the pupils hiding under the beds were dragged out by their feet, while others were perched astride the frames of the cubicles. Justin, the caretaker, bursting in with his revolver, brought an end to this irregular behaviour.

The press got hold of this event, and gave a very lenient account of it as far as the students were concerned. A Paris newspaper faithfully reproduced the nocturnal excesses in a cartoon with the caption: 'Madame la surveillante, nous commémorons la Révolution française. Nous sommes les Fédérés et elles sont les Sans-culottes!' (Madame Supervisor, we are commemorating the French Revolution. We are the Federalists, and they are the *sans-culottes*).

This intrusion into our privacy aroused the indignation of many people, and my father was so incensed that he poured scorn on the 'golden youth' for the simpletons that they were. This is an extract from a letter that I received:

When you started at the Ecole Normale, Madame Stolzenburg said to me: 'Our dormitories are not accessible to men, Monsieur.' I replied, 'I am sure of it, Madame.' I was sincere, but as I did not once ask to see where you were going to spend your nights for the next three years, I cannot imagine how the brigands managed to get in so easily.

If I had foreseen...? That is easy, we would both have come straight back home that same evening. For when I entrusted you to the care of first Madame Renoux and then Madame Stolzenburg, it was a sacred trust that I confided in them.

I imagine that these are not young men who distinguish themselves by their work but, on the contrary, young men of means, scraping through their baccalaureats with difficulty... failures who drag down their university departments with their low intelligence and poor marks.

I received regular letters from my parents: they often wrote at the same time, and although what they wrote about was much the same, their letters were very different. I was touched by my mother's natural prose, which I found very colourful: my father filled up four pages of fine handwriting in a refined style. I have had the good fortune to re-read these letters with much emotion, and in their different ways, they come back to life for me and remind me of the village in the 1930s.

A wedding which took place in the village was a big event and drew a large crowd of onlookers. My mother delighted in telling me the details of the bride's outfit in her direct style:

The bride had a dress made of ottoman (it was rather stiff) with a long train, on her head a hair-net of pearls (it looked like a helmet), all this was not very graceful. But the young girls in dresses of pink *crêpe de chine* and big wide-brimmed hats, made a pretty procession.

In those days, weddings were occasions for celebrations

which went on all day and lasted until the following dawn. We went to them dressed in our finery: the women in long dresses, hatted and gloved: the men in dark suits, some of them in dress suits with satin lapels. The boys would each go to call, at their homes, for the young girls who had been chosen by the bridegroom's family, and would give them a small present. They would be partners for the whole of the ceremony and stay together throughout. A traditional procession escorted the bride to the *mairie* and the church. At midday there would be a sumptuous feast in the large village hall which was decked out for the occasion. Some people preferred to enjoy these banquets in their own surroundings, in their *cave* or an outbuilding; tuns and vats would be draped in large white sheets which were decorated with garlands of foliage and flowers. The many guests would be in excellent mood, for they knew that a *bon coup de fourchette* was in store for them. You can judge for yourself from the following menu, served in Capestang in 1921 at the wedding feast of a cousin, who was born in 1891 and is now the oldest person in the village:

HORS D'OEUVRE
Bouchées à la reine
(Vol au vents filled with chicken)

POISSON
Loup sauce mayonnaise
(Bass in mayonnaise sauce)

ENTREES
Filet de boeuf Richelieu
Salmis de Pigéons
(Fillet of beef 'Richelieu'
Pigeon ragout stewed in a rich brown sauce)

PLAT FROID
Galantine de pintades
(Guinea-fowl galantine)

LEGUMES
Aubergines sauce béchamel

95

ROTI

Dindonneaux
(Young turkeys)

ENTREMETS

Bombe glacée
Pièces Montées
Coupes de fruits
Dessert surfin

VINS

Rouge et Blanc
Champagne

During the meal, compliments, often tedious, had to be conveyed to the happy couple via the children or some backward young girl; the best man, being responsible for entertaining the company, would ask for volunteers to start the singing. There would often be a pianist who was hired for the ball, and the dances were interspersed with games – great pretexts for embraces. A tray would be placed on the ground by a young man who launched it forward with a spinning motion; the young girl who caught it before it fell was allowed to embrace the spinner. Or, couples sitting on their chairs back to back were allowed to clasp each other if their heads turned in the same direction at a given signal; and these diversions always ended with numerous turns of *la danse de l'escargot* in which long lines of young people wound round and round and then uncoiled with great spirit.

Entertainments were rare in the village, so we celebrated the traditional feast days with great enthusiasm, as occasions to enjoy ourselves together were few and far between.

My parents did not enjoy being on their own without me at home in those days. They used to invite their great-nieces and nephews in, and my father was thrilled to see their amazement as they watched the spit being turned. My mother gave them money to buy sweets, but, she wrote to me: 'If they continue to buy chewing-gum which sticks to their insides, I won't give them any more!' Considering how much of it has been consumed since, what damage it must have done!

My mother's kindness to my cousins was well deserved, for they were always ready to help her; Suzanne in particular, from what my mother has told me.

Women did not have the right to vote, but they used to follow the political rows as a form of entertainment.

'At the elections, with Suzanne who acted as my chaperone, I went to listen to the candidates, and we spent quite a time there; when Guilhaumon, the radical candidate, came on, it was more entertaining than the cinema.' And *à propos* the cinema: 'Yesterday I went to see *Marius*. It was very well done. We spent a pleasant evening ... but 4 francs! Once in a while, that's all right!'

My father gave me a review of the performance by the young girls of the village who staged *Ces dames au chapeau vert*:

> On going to bed, the four sisters said goodnight to each other with manic gaiety ... whereas this goodnight, preceded with a kiss on the forehead, should be more respectful, ritual and tender ... in short, a host of details were poor, I noticed.

This was a typical example of his demanding standards.

He also expressed regrets that: 'So many have not been able to experience the wonderful teaching that you have had at school, despite their wish to do so.'

He rejoiced that my future would not be dependent on the price of wine:

> One can say what one likes about *fonctionnaires*; their lives will end up having been exposed to a few ups and downs, but they will never have the same troubles that the winegrowers and small property owners are experiencing at the moment. The civil servants, however humble they may be, at least know where they are going and where their daily bread is coming from.

Sometimes he would become a poet, describing with lyricism

97

the blossoming corner of the garden, and before the Pentecost holidays began: 'Come quickly,' he wrote to me, 'take your share of happiness in the flowers.'

But sometimes I would be subjected to scoldings. Here he demonstrates his aversion to sport: 'Herewith enclosed your wretched Touring Sports' Club form with my signature, but please know that it gives me no pleasure.' He was concerned, moreover, with my *manque de sérieux*. 'Your letter says much, much too much about outings and asking permission for them. We will see about it when the moment comes, and when the holidays, either long or short are not so recent.'

But I received a more severe reprimand, showing how much my eventual inclinations might be held to ridicule:

Since Sunday, we have had a letter addressed to you, from a friend it would seem to me... I do not know whether the feeling is reciprocated, but if it is, I should not wish to be the last to know, only because I absolutely forbid you to keep up a correspondence of which the final consequences can be in no doubt, if I am able to judge from that which I see here. The terms used by this gentleman go remarkably beyond the permitted limits of a simple exchange with a young girl whom one has met in the home of friends: 'Dear Marthe, sweet memory engraved on my heart; I suffer in being so far from you etc., etc.' You must, my girl, forget this message, and put an end to this affair once and for all, even though the distance between you may be thousands of kilometres. Do not take advantage of circumstances which put you out of our control for three-quarters of the year. We do not deserve to be deceived in this way.

My sweetheart was in no immediate danger, as he lived on the Ivory Coast!

You can understand, in the face of such strictness, how paralysed I felt about introducing my chosen one to him.

XII

I did have a few romances, however; the idyll with my friend from the same village had been abruptly broken off by order of his mother, who was alarmed at the ardour of our feelings which ran the risk of getting in the way of his success at the *grandes écoles*. I was 18, and suffered great distress, and threw myself completely into my studies, which resulted in my great success in the *école normale* examination. I do not know whether this thwarted passion affected my boyfriend as much, and threw him into the same studious frenzy, but the fact is that he was admitted into the Polytechnique ... and our paths no longer crossed each other.

That year, in July, I was invited with my cousins, the eldest daughters of my uncle Auguste and my aunt Jeanne, to the *fête* of Saint Geniès des Mourgues, a little village near Lunel. We had to change trains on the way, and by mistake we got into the first class carriages. When we arrived, our descent from the train was particularly noticed, especially by three boys who were at the station, and this made us worthy of the attentive company of partners of the young village jet set for the whole of the festivities!

The *jeux taurins* played a great part in what went on; during the day spirited heifers were let loose in the streets and excited by the crowd which chased after them at full pelt; when the animals came towards us, we nimbly took refuge in a doorway, and this allowed for furtive embraces; on the Sunday the square was encircled by wagons onto which we climbed and sat closely together; in the middle of the arena, agile and intrepid young men tried to lift off the beribboned cockades placed between the heifers' horns; this resulted in falls, spectacular leaps, and either loud boos or applause from the public.

We spent a delightful week at the house of our charming cousins; they were not yet in their 30s and they were in tune with our cheerful spirits. They encouraged our meetings with our escorts, who were thrilled with their hospitality, and this atmosphere, so different from the severity of our families, carried us away a bit.

At our departure, my partner expressed the wish to see me again; he owned a motor car, a luxury most unusual at the time, and he often took the road to Saint-Thibéry. After the holidays, he came to meet me and a friend in Montpellier on the days when I was free. When he became more attentive, I told him that I could only offer him my friendship.

As for my love from the Ivory Coast, I did not behave very well. Having filled him with happiness by giving him high hopes, on his return I had to beg him to give up the joy which I was unable to promise him.

During my second year at the *école normale*, my friend Lucienne painted me an enticing picture of the attractions of the local *fête* which took place in her village at the end of August. As my cousin Margot had been invited, I very much wanted to go with her. I obtained the consent of my father, who entrusted me to the care of a friend with whom he had shared his time in Morocco.

So there we were, the two of us, en route for Capestang. I was entranced, first, by the view from the bus, of Béziers cathedral reflected in the river Orb; it was the first time I had seen that side of the town. Our arrival did not go unnoticed in the village square which was quite full of people at five o'clock in the evening ... strangers! We benefited from this fascinating aura during our stay, with pressing invitations to dance, have coffee and go for walks. It was certainly a splendid *fête*: there were two dance halls with orchestras, and we went tirelessly from one to the other. In the afternoons, all the young set went to the canal: the charm of this spot was a new experience for us: the grass was soft, the shade pleasant, and the atmosphere was merry. As soon as the evening meal was over, there was the battle of the *gisclets*. On a rudimentary stall, Rosine sold sealed tubes of lightly perfumed water, with which the young men sprinkled us copiously. We ran all over the place with shrill cries ... we would have been most disappointed if we had not been chased; but one very forward young man cornered us and drenched us down the inside of our clothes.

We were protected by a waterproof coat, and our hair was tightly crammed under berets. Towards midnight we went to change for the dancing: we wore long dresses and hats during the afternoons. The young men were very properly dressed, and sometimes held a white handkerchief to twine round their partner. I was rather drunk with my conquests, and found it quite normal that the conductor of the orchestra wanted to be introduced to me. To this end he managed to engage the complicity of a third year student at the *école normale*. I found him very attractive and I agreed to go for a walk with him on the wooden bridge. I discovered later that this was the favourite place for lovers to go. I had just met Emile who was the great love of my life. From the dance floor, I used to watch my handsome musician, bent lovingly over his violin from which he coaxed sounds which intoxicated me. I would wait impatiently for the invitation dance; this signalled the interval which freed him for a few moments which were all too short, but enabled us, in a daze, to get to know each other.

I wrote these lines to recall our meeting:

> Dans la nuit qui s'achève
> C'était à Capestang
> J'ai fait un joli rêve.
> J'avais alors vingt ans.
> Tout le village en fête
> En cette nuit d'été
> A l'esprit en goguette,
> Et c'était partout la gaiëté
> Penché sur son violon
> A la terrasse de la 'Grille'
> Il menait le tourbillon
> De tous les garçons et des filles.
> Dans les bras de mon danseur
> J'étais un peu étourdie

En pensant que mon bonheur
Etait bien là pour la vie.

(It happened on a night
At Capestang
That I had a beautiful dream.
I was twenty then.
The village was *en fête*
That summer's night,
In festive mood,
With gaiety all around.
Bent over his violin
On the terrace of the 'Grille',
He led the swirling throng
Of all the boys and girls.
In the arms of my dancing partner
I felt a little dizzy
To realise that there
Was my lifelong happiness.)

I went home filled with wonder at my new joy, and assured of a future illuminated by a great love. This gave me the courage to break off from my ardent colonial; I felt some pangs of remorse, for I had played lightly with his feelings and he was very distressed about it. But the strength of the passion which drew me to Emile had made me realise that the affection I had for him was no more than sisterly.

At the end of the holidays, we found more and more occasions to see each other: most of our meetings took place at Grau d'Agde where I used to go with Margot, chaperoned by my cousin Justine.

Sometimes I would be invited to stay for several days by my aunt Jeanne; she had solved the problem of having reasonably cheap and pleasant holidays for her large family by erecting a wooden hut on the beach, which sheltered a whole crowd during the summer; the comfort was very basic, and we enjoyed a simple outdoor life, away from the usual conveniences. My aunt used to prepare delicious *bouillabaisse* for us, which satisfied our sharpened appetites. My cousins and I lived between the sky and the sea, drunk with our freedom.

I would meet up with Emile where we bathed, but I was under the strict surveillance of my uncle, who used to stand on the beach adjusting his telescope. On Sunday evenings we used to go to the 'Château vert' where there was a band; my aunt, noticing that I always had the same partner, only allowed me to have a few dances, and we had to content ourselves with exchanging glances for the rest of the evening, which I spent dutifully sitting between my chaperones.

In October I went back to my third year at the *école normale*. I was free for a few long exeat Sundays, and Emile used to come to meet me. As was the custom in those days, the countryside or the cinema or theatre screened our restrained passions.

I remember one wonderful day when we went to the municipal theatre to see a production of *Manon*. We had some sublime moments together, thrilling as one under the spell of Massenet's music.

At eight o'clock I would race back to the college, for we tried to prolong our last minutes as much as possible. In between his visits, and via a day pupil who acted as our go-between, I received many letters which grew more and more loving.

I would have been able to go on living in this sweet tranquillity, but I was impatient to share my happiness with my parents.

So I told them about my romance, with much enthusiasm to be sure, emphasising the quality of my lover's musical gifts. The response was scathing: 'You must give up this plan which is nothing more than an infatuation arising from a *jour de fête*.' I should consider building my future with a young man whose profession was the same as mine, which would make sure I had a 'harmonious and contented life'.

What despair I felt, and how I wept!

I made no attempt to defend myself, and I wrote to Emile to tell him that it was all over, there was no appeal. I received letters of outrage, imploring me, and unjust accusations, to which I did not reply.

I called on all my optimism, on the warmth of my friends who gathered round me, and carried on going to *fêtes*, remaining a cheerful and carefree girl; but what misery I felt in my loneliness, and how many times I had to restrain myself from writing all my love to him who, perhaps, had begun to forget me.

My parents in 1910.

My paternal grandparents.

My maternal grandparents with my mother and aunt.

Myself aged about 5, wearing the leather bag and embroidered collar sent by my father from Morocco.

Myself at the Ecole Normale, 1931.

With Margo on the suspension bridge at Saint Thibéry, 1932.

Myself and Emile, 1934.

Myself and Emile, 1942.

Myself and Emile.

The collegiate
church at
Capestang.

Bélet's Jazz 1935.

A scene from 'L'Arlésienne' 1944.

1946 My class at the infant school.

1949 The Capestang town band.

Emile in full song.

The Last Rites of an Austere Life

2nd Movement – Allegro molto ritmato

XIII

Some time later, I woke up one morning feeling out of sorts; I was running a slight temperature, and was admitted to the sick bay; this did not upset me very much, I was even quite glad, for that day I had been appointed to give the model lesson to the school next door: we used to dread this ordeal, and I was a bit worried that my classmates would accuse me of skiving out of it!

Next day, the 5th of May, I was taken home by taxi, and there began a very bad attack of typhoid fever, a long period of anguish for my parents, unlimited devotion from all the family, and an ordeal during which I struggled between life and death. In those days the treatment of the disease was not easy: several baths a day (fortunately my home was well equipped), followed with being packed round with ice, which makes me shiver to remember. I sank into unconsciousness.

I was a very difficult patient; I could never abide milk, and whenever anyone approached my lips with it, I would tip it over the bedclothes with a flick of the hand. I was grudgingly given some orange juice to quench my thirst.

On the Sunday of Pentecost, I was given the last rites, and apparently all the church congregation in the village offered fervent prayers that a young girl of 20 years old should be saved. Both the doctor and the priest were of the opinion that I had reached the bourne of the beyond.

I have since heard, on the television, evidence from people who, having been in a coma, tell of extraordinary recollections of this short period 'outside life'. To be truthful, I have absolutely no memory of it, except that, during this long period of unconsciousness, I saw into my future destiny, living through my working life as a teacher at Capestang,

107

beside him whom my subconscious kept secret. I remember it very distinctly, and I had confirmation of it in a letter from Margot to Emile: 'In her delirium, she talks of her class at Capestang!' A premonition caused by such a strong desire!

I emerged from this nightmare after 73 days of struggle, having lost a lot of weight, but with a renewed taste for life. My weak legs gave way under me when I tried to walk, and it was in the arms of my cousin Justine (I weighed so little), that I looked round once more at the rooms of my home, going into raptures over everything. From my balcony I marvelled at the garden full of flowers, and the roses had never seemed so beautiful!

Lamartine wrote:

> Au regard d'un mourant le soleil est si beau.
> (To a dying man, the sun looks so beautiful.)

How can one describe the splendour of a beautiful day in July, flooding with joy a convalescent who is emerging from a tunnel where everything was in darkness!

Gradually my parents helped me to recover my physical strength; I had to learn to walk again, and my voice which had been completely inaudible during the last month of my illness, came back very slowly.

Little by little, so as not to upset me, I was told the story of this long agony, recalling how my family had helped my poor parents, and the makeshift measures they had at their disposal. Serious complications had followed one upon another to the despair of my young doctor; he even began to think that death would be preferable to survival without my mental faculties. I read all the letters written to my parents and I was touched by so much interest and concern. The memory of Emile came back to me and I was afraid to speak of it. At the right moment, Margot told me that they had been writing to each other since the beginning of my illness. I was moved and happy to know that he still loved me, and I wrote to him to express my faithfulness and tell him how desperate I felt at having to renounce our happiness.

This encouraged him to be bold enough to write to my

father; perhaps he was clumsy, for this attempt hardened the parental refusal.

I was still in bed when the headmistress of the *école normale*, accompanied by her niece, came to see me; this show of concern deeply touched my parents. When, in October, I went to pass the third part of the *Brevet supérieur*, she said to me: 'My child, your recovery is the miracle of science and of love.'

Day after day, she had followed the course of my illness from weekly letters from my father which she read out to my classmates.

Her visit caused me such powerful feelings that the next day I had a relapse; it was the 14th of July and my father was conducting the concert which had to be interrupted – my health problems were publicly revealed; certainly I lacked discretion.

This ordeal showed me the fragility of existence and made me aware of what a marvellous gift life is. As it has been prolonged miraculously for me, I must be worthy of it and always try to make myself available for others.

* * *

I benefited from five months' absence of study, and I had excellent results in the exam which finalised my training as a teacher. As I have said already, I had a gift for exams, calmly summoning all my energy and, certainly, plenty of luck. Is that why my first post was ... Montpellier? This appointment did not please me: I dreamed of a post in the mountains, only picturing the life of the peasants and the joy of developing the minds of the children of all ages, for whom the school-teacher is a salvation. Later on, letters from my friends, teaching in deprived hamlets, told me of their difficult life in the destitute schools, the discomfort of their living arrangements, and their isolation because of the snow from November to March!

This appointment in the main town did not please my father either; he was anxious about me being set loose in a big city.

He entrusted me to a retired couple he knew, where I was looked after and thoroughly cosseted. In contrast, he was enthusiastic about the establishment which would be my first testing ground.

109

The Ecole Maternelle Docteur Roux, newly built, had recently opened its doors and was entitled, with reason, to be called the department's model school: it was provided with the most up to date equipment, in light and artistically decorated classrooms. The areas for games and relaxation, recently created, were wonderfully adapted for their purpose. I was dazzled by such richness of facilities, and with their possibilities. The playground, full of flowers, looked very different from the usual dreary recreation grounds.

The luxury and comfort of the buildings were not the only reasons for my euphoria; my only other colleague there was the headmistress herself, Mademoiselle Maraval, an outstanding person who gained all my admiration and feeling of compatibility immediately. Like Mireille of the *école annexe*, she had a very high standard of ability and a love of her job plus being always cheerful and with a zest for life and *la fête*...

Far from being disappointed, she was delighted to have at her side a young teacher fresh from the *école normale*. She put me in charge of the older children, where, she said, I would have more chance of being appreciated. I had everything I needed to do the job really well; Mademoiselle Maraval helped me with her wise counsel, and rejoiced in my enthusiasm and my desire to learn. In spite of all this, I was quite apprehensive; the new and perfect equipment, the lay-out of the school, and the personality of the headmistress prompted frequent visits from inspectors and notables concerned with education, and I was conscious of my weaknesses and lack of experience.

After school, Mademoiselle Maraval would invite me to her apartment where we would join her friend, a teacher at the primary school; they took obvious pleasure in my company, and enjoyed my spontaneity and enthusiasm; they were very generous with the little treats they gave me. Their affection for me continued well beyond my stay with them, with a regular correspondence and presents on many an occasion.

I would have been very happy had the memory of Emile not been there to torture me. I used to get news of him from my friend Lucille of Capestang, who wrote and told me how sad and distraught he was.

Luckily I had my work to occupy my mind. The people with whom I was staying had nothing to worry about as far as looking after my morals was concerned; I had no wish to enjoy the delights of the town, and I worked hard so as not to disappoint Mademoiselle Maraval.

* * *

At Christmas, quite contrary to my wishes, I heard of my new post... I had to change places with the headmistress of the infant school at Montagnac; this village, which was near my own, was convenient for me, but ... Headmistress! I cried about it for two whole days ... I felt little prepared for this responsibility, and it frightened me.

Accompanied, as usual, by my father, I arrived at my new post; we were received by the headmistress, Mademoiselle C. who was the daughter of a minister, and wore very severe clothes; she was stiff in her black dress, and her hair was scraped back in a little bun. I learned later of Mademoiselle Maraval's anger at having to take on her new assistant. In her letters she made constant complaints about her coldness and mundane character.

The surroundings resembled her: dreary, bare walls, dark tables cluttered with wooden bricks and slates, which, with a few exercise books and coloured crayons, made up the sum total of the equipment. I was dumbfounded, and my father could not stop himself from saying: 'Mademoiselle, you are going to go up in the world ... but what a downfall for *her!*'

On the first day of the new term, I met my assistant, much older than I was, and afflicted with a severe limp; she was a very nice person, full of good will, but not suitable for an infant school. She was absolutely terrified of the Inspector who was quite harsh with her, something I could understand when I saw how she handled the little ones' class. The cleaner, Madame C., was not very affable; a sturdy woman with a stern appearance, she had lived in constant dissension with my predecessor, and they had actually come to blows...

In this scarcely exhilarating environment, I spent a happy stay, thanks to my optimism and enthusiasm for my work. I livened up the classrooms with brightly coloured friezes, changed the lay-out of the furniture and got rid of the dreary

111

slates. But how was I going to occupy my little pupils without teaching materials?

I called upon the generosity of the craftsmen and shop-keepers, collecting cardboard boxes, tins, books of wallpaper samples, samples of leather, material etc., ... I had a large apartment in which the few pieces of furniture bought by my parents seemed lost, and I cluttered up one whole room with all my finds. Late into the night I cut up, I glued, I made designs for sensory games or pictures for reading material ... but it was still not enough. So I decided to go to the *mairie* and ask for a grant for the purchase of supplies. The municipal personnel were amazed to hear what was needed; I think they rated the infant school as a mere day-nursery. I had to make so many approaches to the mayor, a bachelor doctor, that word got round of our marriage!

We got on very well together and I won my case; educational games and toys, paintbrushes, paints, large sheets of drawing paper, and material for handicrafts were stocked up in a store cupboard, and individual drawers contained beads; sticky letters and numbers were placed around the classroom. I loved watching the children's wonder as they threw colours onto the big drawing sheets fixed to the wall, and their joy in the open air rhythmic exercises which I accompanied on my mandolin.

I experienced some of the greatest joys of my professional teaching life during these two years, for everything was new for the children, and I stretched myself to the limits of my knowledge to fulfil their needs.

For the first time, the school had a celebration at Christmas: with a portion of my salary, which was not very high, I bought a toy for each child – a very modest one, to be sure, but received with so much delight: I remember that my present for the little girls was a pink celluloid doll's pram, eight centimetres long with a minute baby doll inside, made of rubber. This seems very paltry compared to what children have today, but I am sure that my little girls treasured their presents, and the mothers were very touched.

In July, The Association of Non-Denominational Schools, which was very active on account of the competition from the sectarian schools, held a huge public *fête*: my children took part in it with singing and dancing, and this innovation was much appreciated.

A few months after my installation we had the visit from the Inspector, Madame Des, who was particularly exacting. I think that her kindness towards me was the result of having heard of me from Mademoiselle Maraval whom she held in high esteem.

The atmosphere of the school had changed as well as the decor; I had succeeded in modifying slightly the narrow way in which Madame B. occupied her *petits*; we sang together, and even our cleaner, Madame C., who had a very lovely voice, joined in our songs and dances.

All this engendered an enthusiasm amongst the mothers for what went on in the school; they responded willingly to my appeals for help, and gave a hand in the preparation of festive occasions.

This unbounded activity helped a little to anaesthetise the underlying pain, which was always there, of my frustrated longing; my thoughts often turned to him, and he was also yearning, but neither he nor I dared to infringe my father's prohibition.

XIV

But one day ... at the end of school, the caretaker announced that a commercial traveller had come to see me ... and I found myself face to face with Emile, a leather briefcase in his hand and a violin tucked under his arm. To justify his absence to his parents he had given the pretext that he was playing for a dance at a wedding.

More than a year had passed since our last meeting, and we had gone through the painful ordeal of my illness! After greeting each other again with great dignity (mercifully my pupils were too young to detect my turmoil) it was with wild abandon and much feeling that we fell into each other's arms once we were alone together in my apartment.

During this long time of solitude he had sent me a ballad composed especially for me, in a minor key. Here are the words:

> Ne jamais la voir ni l'entendre
> Ne jamais tout haut la nommer
> Mais fidèle toujours l'attendre
> Toujours l'aimer.
>
> Ouvrir les bras et las d'attendre
> Sur le néant les refermer
> Mais encore toujours les lui tendre
> Toujours l'aimer.
>
> Ah! ne pouvoir que les lui tendre
> Et dans les pleurs se consumer
> Mais ces pleurs toujours répandre
> Toujours l'aimer.

114

(Never to see nor hear her,
Never to speak her name,
But ever faithful I await her
Loving her always the same.

To open my arms, tired of waiting,
On nothing to close them again,
But ever still open them for her
Loving her always the same.

Ah! unable to open them to her,
In tears I languish and wane
But my tears continue just falling
Loving her always the same.)

Before he left, I did not have the courage to refuse him other visits, and we met up again on Thursdays for a few hours in Pézénas or Montpellier; I was too well known in Montagnac.

Certainly we were happy to see each other again, and each time more in love, but the uncertainty of our future hovered over this joy.

I felt torn apart during these meetings; guilty towards my parents whose trust in me I was betraying, and on the other hand I blamed myself for encouraging a passion the outcome of which I could not predict.

My father's health was deteriorating rapidly – the doctor had warned me that he had a weak heart, and I feared the consequences of a painful confrontation. His worsened condition made it necessary to be at his bedside constantly during the long holidays. On 1st October I returned to my beloved school, happy that my father seemed to be getting better, as he was taking up his activities again very gently, and had recovered his taste for his passion for music, listening to the musical broadcasts on the radio which my first salary had enabled me to give him.

I enjoyed going back to my parents every Sunday (I never had a free Saturday). Before the first weekend, I had an unfortunate accident: a heavy clock which was badly fixed to the classroom wall fell on my head. So I arrived home with a swollen face all the colours of the rainbow. Whether it was my appearance that alarmed my father I do not know, but the fact remains that after I had gone, he said to my mother: 'That little girl doesn't look at all well!' This remark provoked my mother to let out a long suppressed flash of 'As long as you forbid her to see that young man from Capestang, she will not recover.' My father, astonished and bowled over by the strength of this romance which he believed to be over and done with, declared immediately: 'If that's where her happiness lies, I do not wish to oppose it; she shall have the life she has chosen. I think that next Saturday, this happy news will restore her spirits.'

The following Thursday I attended the marriage service of one of my friends at Pézénas; during the ceremony, for some unaccountable reason, I was overcome with a feeling of anguish. On my arrival back at Montagnac for lunch, I learned that I was wanted at home; my father's condition had suddenly worsened. I arrived to learn that he had been struck down by a bout of emphysema.

He had struggled until noon which was the time the bus arrived from Pézénas, hoping that perhaps ... but fate had not decreed that he should have the joy of giving me great happiness. I felt a little guilty: if I had dared to stand up for our mutual feelings, he might perhaps have given in earlier?

It was beside his lifeless body that my mother told me of his consent. I was outraged by this fateful coincidence, which seemed too hard to bear, and at first I swear I could not believe it: happily, many witnesses amongst friends and relations, whom my mother, rejoicing, had told of my father's change of heart, removed my doubts.

Emile, told at one and the same time of my father's changed attitude and of his death, was able to attend his funeral; this was marked by the emphasis on music which he had served with so much devotion, and Emile was there for the moving homage which was paid him. My father was 55 years old!

I never bore him any resentment; I have missed him very much at times; I always had a great filial devotion for him which I pass down to my offspring in telling them about the exceptional man who was their grandfather.

A fortnight after the death of my father, Emile came, with his mother, to ask for my hand. That day, so long awaited,

which fills with joy all couples in love, was spent in tears ...
but it marked the end of a long and painful wait, and we were
happy, at long last, to be able to see each other freely.

My mother followed me to Montagnac; this change in her
life helped her a great deal in coping with her grief. Outside
school hours we were always together; my living quarters
were in the school building, and my neighbours on the same
floor were delightful.

Like me, my mother certainly would have wished to
prolong this stay if the situation with Emile had not meant my
asking for a change of post; I looked for it without much
enthusiasm, and I gathered all the children's mothers together
to tell them of my decision. We were all moved; they clubbed
together to give me a superb leaving present, and some
families came to Saint-Thibéry to bring me personal souvenirs: 'You have done so much for our children!' I have never
forgotten the time in that hospitable village, nor the faces of
the children – who are now grandparents – for whom I put so
much energy into renovating the school.

Our marriage took place on 7th August 1935: it was in the
morning, at a short ceremony, as both our mothers had lost
their husbands. Our paternal grandparents were there, with
my uncles and aunts, and my girl cousins had had the
kindness to accompany me in their best clothes. I had bought
(for just one hour's wear!) a wedding dress, which I put aside
for my sad mourning clothes before setting off on our honey-
moon. Emile's cousins accompanied us to Agde station, and I
movingly recall the ardour with which my new husband
clasped me to him in the empty compartment, saying 'At last!'

We went towards the Pyrénées; having bought a round-trip
ticket, we could take the train in a different direction each day,
in the area between Toulouse and Hendaye. For three weeks
we tired ourselves out criss-crossing this region, wanting to
see all of it, when it would have been more sensible to choose
a pleasant spot to stay, and savour our happiness.

We brought back many photographs of all our stops, which
bring back wonderful memories.

In September, I was told of my appointment to the primary
school in Capestang. I felt fortunate compared to my friends,
exiled to mountain hamlets. We used to exchange lots of news

in letters to one another, and the AUE group to which I used to belong had instituted the *circulante*, a collection of letters which went out to each one of us in our new lives. We welcomed the envelope joyfully when it arrived; it contained seven letters, to which we added our own, taking out the earliest one which was from the classmate to whom we sent off the collection next: this was an excellent initiative, and this interesting correspondence, rich with our varied characters, must have brought warmth to the loneliness.

In this way, my friends disclosed the difficulties of their lives: snow for a great part of the year, rough and ready accommodation, difficulty in obtaining provisions. Sometimes they were able to get over their isolation by meeting up together, making difficult journeys on a bicycle or on foot. They showed much faith in the profession by carrying on teaching in poorly equipped classrooms, with children whose ages ranged from five to twelve, often kept at home to look after the cows or help with work on the farm ... but how exhilarating it must have been to open out new and exciting horizons to these children who lived in such a restricted world! In 1933, travel was rare, and the male population only left their home surroundings to do military service.

Nowadays these posts no longer exist for novice teachers; the schools have closed, and in many cases the little village has not survived this loss. Our *circulante* has passed away with the years. Why didn't we keep it going? It would have been invaluable in the times of sorrow, which each of us, in turn, has been through.

Despite my wishes having been granted, I did not welcome the announcement of my transfer with transports of joy.

XV

I missed my little school in Montagnac, and I was distressed at inflicting another move on my mother. My living arrangements in the village did not exactly fill me with euphoria; this important canton was very behind the times as far as community facilities were concerned. The houses had no running water, and one had to get what one needed for oneself, either from the outlets from the canal (not fit for drinking), or from the fountains for drinking water. Nor were these conveniently situated; in the garage of the house we had rented, we installed a slop pail under a commode behind a screen. This tremendously useful utensil – heavens! – was emptied every morning by the latrine man, who went through the village streets; he was a very nice fellow who stopped at each junction where the neighbourhood buckets were rounded up, and had no qualms about eating his mid-day meals while sitting astride his barrel.

Doing the washing became a real drudgery, and we dried our laundry on a line stretched along the outside wall.

We had never experienced living in such discomfort and my mother found it difficult to adjust to this sort of life.

Most of the rich landowners were idle, strolling through their vines to supervise their toiling labourers; the workers, in contrast, had to slave for a very long working day to make the most of the few small plots of vines that they could afford, and the memory of the severe strike of 1933 still haunts the minds of these people.

There were few representatives of the middle class. I was surprised at how many women and girls rode bicycles; I learned later that this mode of transport was essential for their daily journey into the countryside where they were employed.

119

This sort of existence was very different from life in my village, which mostly consisted of small landowners, living on the income from their vines and only drawing on female labour for collecting up the vine shoots, a little bit of manuring, and at harvest time. The appearance of the streets marked the different strata which existed in the population: beautiful *maisons de maîtres*, surrounded by gardens, were juxtaposed with small, mean homes which often looked neglected.

In the first years of my work there, I was not treated with the same respect that had surrounded me in my first post; *fonctionnaires*, of whom I was one, were considered as belonging to a privileged class, and there was jealousy around for various reasons. This was in 1935! All this has completely changed since, and become more standardised; the rich bosses have almost all disappeared, the workers have acquired a more comfortably off way of life, and a real effort with planning has been undertaken in the town.

Coming from a wine-growing village made up of medium or small landowners, I was surprised at the life of ease led by the big landowners in Capestang. Every Friday, they used to go to Béziers where the wine auction was held. The main artery of this town, the Allées Paul Riquet, was a meeting place, much frequented by groups of extremely well-dressed men, talking vigorously, but also spending a lot of time in the smart cafés and restaurants in the town; the Grand Café Glacier in the main street which has now lost its glory of those years, and the Trou Normande which served the finest menus. These gentlemen regularly went to gamble in the Casino at Valras, a nearby bathing resort. All these pleasures were seldom enjoyed with their wives, the ladies' lives being confined to an unrelieved pattern of their home and the church.

For the most part, these gentlemen were not satisfied with the routine of married life. Many of them kept mistresses whom they supported in a very grand manner. The regular trips into the town furnished convenient excuses to enjoy these fringe pleasures. Divorce was rare in those days, but what hypocrisy was hidden in the respectability of these bourgeois marriages. It seemed that the wives took little

120

offence at these customs; it was a part of the 'standing', and showed the stringency of their own intimate relations, limited to the necessity of conception.

So their spouses devoted themselves to it all joyfully; their indolence and financial means allowed them some eccentricities; I was told that they rented carriages from the SNCF at Béziers, in which to carry on their affairs with accommodating ladies on their way to Toulouse where they would go and have parties.

Toulouse was *the* place to go for many of this *bourgeoisie*; for shopping and for clothes, and for religious institutions where young girls were sent to boarding school at a very early age. There they found a certain degree of comfort, and even a few rules of hygiene, but they used to take their baths dressed in a long nightgown to cover the 'shameful' parts of their bodies! Some families thought it more refined, particularly between 1920 and 1930, to send their children to convents in Spain.

All this shows what luxury the bourgeois wine-growers enjoyed; the display of this wealth explains the resentment suppressed by the workers, and the explosion of the rebellion in 1933.

However, side by side with these examples of arrogance, it was also in these families that one found evidence of a deeply cultural life: a close collaboration with Castelbon de Beauxhostes made for some glorious performances in the arena at Béziers, and there was correspondence with Mistral, the great Provençal poet. Photographic records prove that they took part with Marcellin Albert in the defence of the wine industry of southern France, in the literary demonstrations of Mistral and the artistic life of the region, with Lucyle Panis of the Opéra de Paris.

This extravagant and leisured lifestyle did not survive the exigencies of the modern world, and often ended in misery; most of these people were financially ruined, their sumptuous homes changed ownership, and their descendants left the village.

*   *   *

Capestang and the surrounding area used to be served by the railway line. Built in 1923, it aroused great protests: in

particular the smoke was deemed to have a harmful effect on
the bunches of grapes ... and on the quality of the wine!...

The *Revue du Cercle* recalls the slowness of this method of
transport:

> Le train marchait si rapidement
> Que notre notaire, homme charmant
> A pu rédiger trois testaments...
> Et qu'une femme eut juste le temps
> D'accoucher de deux beaux enfants.

> (The train travelled at such a speed
> That our charming *notaire*
> Managed to draw up three wills,
> And a woman just had time
> To give birth to two splendid babies.)

The village presented very contrasting aspects. Thanks to the
support from the municipality, Capestang was in the forefront
for the teaching of music. Political rivalries having been calmed
down, the town band reassembled all the musicians, of whom
there were a considerable number; the conductor and the
assistant conductor gave free tuition to the young, who were
even lent musical instruments. Thus music has always been a
part of life in Capestang, and other communities have envied
us for it. Today this honour is in great danger; the number of
musicians is fewer, and the young people disdain wind and
brass instruments in favour of the piano. We are witnessing the
lingering death of the wind orchestra.

Some completed projects were greatly appreciated, such as
the provision of public baths (with showers) which made up for
the lack of running water in the village. But there was still no
main drainage, which we had to wait for until 1965. In order
that their families could drink pure, fresh water, the women,
armed with jugs, went to the Théron fountain where spring
water flowed which had been harnessed from a nearby hill:

> Au Pech, venez quand meurt le jour,
> Je dors la nuit, presque sans voiles,
> Le seul manteau de mes atours

Ou la rosée met son velours
C'est le manteau d'or des étoiles

('La nymphe du Théron – *Revue du Cercle*)

(Come to the fountain as the twilight falls,
I sleep the night almost naked,
The only covering I have around me
Is the golden cloak of the stars
When the rosy sky puts on its velvet coat)

One had to go down some steps to get to the tap, which still works today. This shady corner made an ideal trysting place:

'Je suis toute vérdie de mousse
A l'instant je quitte ma source
Et je titube d'émotion...
Mes marches sont un peu falotes
Et ma rampe par trop vieillotte
En soutint des générations!
En ai-je vu des jouvencelles
Courir vers moi jeunes et belles
Accompagnées de jeunes fous!
Soupirs confus ... rires sonores ...
Baisers qui font les yeux se clore.
En ai-je vu des rendez-vous!'
(*Revue du Cercle*)

(I am all green with moss
When I leave my spring,
And I stumble with emotion...
My steps are a little uneven,
And my handrail looks worn
From the use of generations!
What damsels I have seen,
Running towards me, young and beautiful,
Together with wild youths!
Confused sighs ... loud laughter...
Kisses so deep they close the eyes.
What rendez-vous I have witnessed!)

123

Lovers also used to go to the canal, which bordered the top end of the village. It was a much frequented walk under the lovely lines of plane trees; the fishermen would be settled on the soft grassy banks studded with daisies, their eyes fixed on their floats ... In summer throughout the afternoons, on Sunday evenings, and on holidays, the banks of the canal took on the atmosphere of a fair. Escaping from the heat of the village streets, entire families came to take advantage of the pleasant cool of the water; seated on rugs spread out on the grass, they would enjoy a grill cooked on the spot, and the provisions they had brought along in a wicker basket. It was a popular pastime, looked forward to impatiently by the children, as they learned to swim very early, and their great pride was to be able to swim across to the other side of the canal.

Nowadays, its banks are neglected, the young people prefer to go by car on trips to the seaside, and the old ones let themselves be seduced by the programmes on television ... Our canal is only enlivened by the numerous barges, flying foreign flags, which take out peaceable boaters who, even though far from their own homes, know how to come and enjoy the special charm of this beautiful spot.

Another feature of the place is the *étang* from which the village gets its name. It stretches out at the lower end into a vast plain which only floods in the rainy season. In those days it was still plentifully stocked with fish which abounded in the conduits which ran along it, disappearing between the *canottes*. One used to be able to catch plenty of mullet, carp, eels and pike. The fishermen themselves maintained the resource by stocking the streams which flowed into this lake. The authors of the *Revue du Cercle* wrote of the 'Sirène de l'Etang', who looked after this wild habitat, and thus described her realm:

'Dès que le jour paraît à l'horizon vermeil
J'offre mon corps lascif aux baisers du soleil
Les saules paresseux me donnent leur ombrage
Dans le vol des oiseaux, je cherche des présages
Et j'écoute, alanguie, quand meurt le soleil d'or
La rainette qui chante auprès de l'eau qui dort;

Lorsques des flots, enfin, sous les yeux d'Ensérune,
Je sors enamourée, toute argentée de lune,
C'est pour mieux me blottir, après quelques plongeons,
Dans mon nid de canottes ou dans un nid de joncs...'

(When day dawns in the crimson sky
I offer my lusting body to the sun's kisses,
The indolent willows give me their shade
And I look for portents in the flight of birds;
Languidly I listen, as the sun goes down,
To the tree-frog singing by the sleeping water;
When the flood-tide comes, at last, under the gaze of
    Ensérune,
I rise, besotted, silvered in the moonlight,
The better to snuggle, after several dives,
Into my cane bed, or my nest of rushes.)

Under cover of darkness, the frogs used to be tracked down
by torchlight to increase the profits gained from the *étang*. This
plentiful source of food was particularly appreciated during
the restrictions of the last war.

Night-time hunting for water fowl also took place, a tradition which still has its followers today. In the darkness,
the *étang* is alive with the sounds of its wild life. This is how a
hunter poet, Henri Granier, described them:

'...Je peux distinguer
La percussion des foulques en un vrai xylophone,
Le rire du plongeon, le hibou chuinter.
Pendant que le butor pète dans le trombone,
Une dame colvert trompette quelque part.
La mignonne sarcelle essaie la clarinette
Alors que son mari, toujours aussi bavard
Fais resonner partout son sifflet à roulette
Jusqu'au petit matin, quand l'ombre se dissipe,
Ce concert naturel me comble et me ravit...'

(...I can hear
A xylophone in the percussion of the coots,
The laugh of the diver, the hoot of the owl.

125

While the bittern sounds off like the trombone,
A female mallard trumpets somewhere.
The sweet teal tries the clarinet,
While her mate, ever-talkative,
Makes his whistle echo everywhere.
Until the early morning and the end of night
This natural concert fills me with delight...)

Warmly dressed for a long vigil in the *gabions*, hides fixed up on piles, the hunters carefully place their *appelants*, which are ducks paddling in the water but with one foot tied down, and destined to call down the wild fowl by their cries. These come to join their fellows, little suspecting the presence of the men lying in wait for them, and are shot down by the guns which shatter the silence of the night. But sometimes the hunter has a sensitive soul and the poet in him feels some remorse for his victims:

Ils palpitent encore et tout çela me navre
Je me suis pas très fier de mon geste meutrier
Mais je suis satisfait de mon tableau de chasse.
Allez donc expliquer cette contradiction
De l'âme du chasseur, de ce vilain rapace,
Devant tant de beauté, rempli de contrition.

(They are still fluttering, and all this grieves me,
I feel no great pride in my slaughtering
But I am content with my bag.
Can you explain this paradox to me,
How the soul of the hunter, this predatory villain,
In the face of such beauty, can fill with remorse?)

* * *

I found Capestang certainly going through changing times. The appeal of the social life of the past had gone: the memory of the painful strike of 1933 was still very much around, and explained the aggressiveness of the population. The agricultural workers, badly paid by the owners who were making comfortable profits, had stopped all work just at the moment of the copper sulphate spraying – a treatment necessary to

126

safeguard the harvest. The intervention of the armed forces created a rebellious climate. In spite of assistance many families went hungry, and the dreadful hardships were not forgotten ... The cultural and artistic life had not stood up to this test. Only the 'Cercle', which united the wealthy wine-growers, survived until 1939.

Before this period, Capestang was a fortunate village in this respect.

Subject to the socio-economic divisions imposed by wealth, there were three Societies which livened up the town, each one putting on a variety of evening entertainments three times a year.

'Les Amusaires' had a workers' membership; the middle class belonged to 'L'Aurore Littéraire', and the affluent made up the 'Cercle'. There was spirited competition between the three groups, and the shows were of a high standard, with singers, sketches, plays in the Occitan language by Emile Barthe, and comedies by Comteline, Feydeau and Labiche.

'L'Aurore' even risked producing the complete light opera, *Les Cloches de Corneville*, a proof that there were excellent voices in the society. This rather *bourgeois* group had a well stocked library for the use of its members.

The evenings provided by the 'Cercle' demonstrated a higher level of culture; in 1924 a revue in verse was staged, full of poetry and humour, recalling life in Capestang after the 1914 war. This was the prelude to it:

Place à nos rimailleurs et vive la démence
Car ce sont tous des gars du Midi de la France
 Le pays du soleil!
Et si leur poesie de Rostand n'est égale
C'est qu'ils ont copié le chant de leurs cigales
 Dans les matins vermeils.

(Make way for our rhymesters, and long live their
 lunacy,
For these are all lads from the sunny
 French Midi!
And if their poetry is not up to Rostand's
It's because they have copied the song of their crickets
 In the rosy dawn.)

127

The shows put on by the 'Aurore' and the 'Cercle' took place in the Café de la Grille, which was the most popular of the six establishments at the time. 'Les Amusaires' made do with a *cave* fitted out for the purpose.

The audiences were made up of people from the same class as the actors; sometimes, however, the members of the 'Aurore' would mingle with the workers, but it was out of the question for the latter to be admitted to the 'Cercle' where dinner jackets and evening dress were *de rigueur*.

My husband had the good fortune to play in all three societies, where they used his gifts as a comedian, actor and violinist to full advantage.

The shows, which were free, had to have several performances, as they had a great following, and the halls were not very big.

Apart from this, two separate musical societies grew up in the village because of the political divisions. There was 'la musique de droit' which performed for the religious ceremonies, and 'la musique de gauche' which took part in the republican celebrations. A certain animosity existed between these two bands, and making a mockery of the old saying *la musique adoucit les moeurs*, famous battles where musical instruments were used as weapons actually broke out in the village square! I was told about this by my husband's grandfather, who had also taken part in other memorable frays: emulating the heroes of Louis Pergaud's *La Guerre des Boutons*, the children of Capestang and Puisserguier, villages four kilometres apart, let out their aggression by meeting regularly in the countryside between the two, to bombard each other with stones. There were epic battles between the 'Manja escarpàs' and the 'Manjadoires', the respective nicknames of the two clans ('Big carp eaters' and 'Gluttons').

Gone now too are the beautiful Sunday evenings in summer, when the majority of the population used to gather in the square, enlarged by the municipality as soon as the Great War was over to enhance the imposing Collégiale – the pride of the citizens of Capestang. It was in the square that we used to go to the open-air cinema, which showed serialised silent films with a musical accompaniment provided by a violinist and a

128

blind pianist, much esteemed for the part they played in the religious and artistic life of the village.

In 1926, tired of classical orchestras made up of violins, clarinets, tubas and strings playing polkas, reels, mazurkas and waltzes, the young people called for new rhythms and new sounds. Hearing what they were saying, Emile modified his music group and introduced melodic jazz with new instruments: piano, saxophones, cornet (soon replaced by the trumpet), and percussion, but he kept the violin. The dances changed their rhythm and their names: one-step, foxtrot, java, tango – but the waltz withstood all the developments. At this time, Capestang was in the avant-garde for modern music in the region.

At the school, I was kindly welcomed, but I was out of step with my colleagues, who were much older than I was.

My little seven- and eight-year-old pupils were sweet, and I was very involved there, but I think I was too demanding, and some mothers complained of my strictness. Some of my attempts were not exactly successful. When teaching my little girls to recite *'Minet boit son lait'*, I wanted to make it a lifelike presentation; I brought in a young cat in a hamper containing a saucer and a bottle of milk. I told my intrigued pupils that I had a surprise for them. Carefully, I opened the basket; the little cat leapt out and squeals and laughter burst out in the classroom; terrified, the pussy-cat jumped to safety through the window which, stupidly, had been left open. There was I in a right predicament: my children over-excited, my cat escaped (I had 'borrowed' it from a neighbour) ... luckily, a nice young man rescued it with the aid of a ladder, from where it had taken refuge on a nearby roof. I had to confess my mishap to my headmistress, who made fun of my methods:

'Ah! Madame Bélet, what silly things you do in the name of down-to-earth teaching. When you tell them about cows, will you bring one of those into the class too?'

Another amusing memory I have is of an exercise in conjugation. With great care, Joséphine wrote:

Nous cueillons les pâquerettons
Vous cueillez les pâquerettez!!

129

Emile came into the school regularly to teach music and singing, and if it was playtime when he came through the gate, the 'big ones' would nudge each other with their elbows to see my face turn crimson.

We used to go and eat with Emile's family every Sunday; there we would meet up with my mother-in-law and his paternal grandparents. Grandfather Paul's philosophy encouraged him to lead a contented life of ease, with a cigarette in his lips, and Finette, whom he had married at the age of 18, at his side. 'She was so pretty,' he said, 'that I was afraid someone else would take her from me.'

Grandmother was an old lady with a very fine face, always smiling and gentle. Nothing disturbed her good humour, not even the lively escapades of her daughter-in-law. She used to be renowned for her work as an ironer, and when I knew her she used to help my mother-in-law to make *galines*, hats made of material stretched over willow twigs, which fitted the head closely, and the women wore them out in the countryside to protect themselves both from the cold and the heat.

Because of the premature loss of their son, this delightful old couple had transferred all their affection onto Emile. They must have been very unhappy when our mutual love was thwarted. Thus they gave me doubly of their kindness, grateful for the happiness I gave to the person they cherished so much.

Sundays were not bright spots in my life at Capestang. In the afternoon, my mother-in-law dragged my mother and me off to call on her friends who served us coffee with little cakes amid a lot of chatter. I did not dare to shirk these visits which were hardly thrilling for a young woman. During these times, my husband was conducting the orchestra at the Café de la Grille for the young people to dance to. He had not given up this demanding and poorly paid job, as my mourning forbade us to go out anywhere.

When a suitable time had elapsed for us to be able to enjoy ourselves, we used to go to the afternoon show at the local cinema; in the interval, Marie, the wife of the film-operator, used to sell long, brightly coloured barley-sugar twists, and we used to enjoy meeting up with the same regular audience.

We would sit in the gallery right next to the projection-room, unconscious of any danger; I learnt later that there was only a soda siphon available in case of a fire! We were ignorant of safety standards then: our greatest delight was to take refuge in our empty house after the show and enjoy our moments of intimacy, which felt like the taste of forbidden fruit: our married life was always hindered by the constant presence of our mothers. We could not even enjoy ourselves alone together in the sweet calm of the evenings; Emile was occupied every evening with music classes or rehearsals with the *harmonie*; I used to prepare my lessons to the rhythm of the clicking of our mothers' knitting needles.

At that time, accompanying my mother, who found it a bit difficult to walk, to Sunday mass, I watched a strange scene take place in the church: a woman, imposing in her size and the elegance of her dress, went up the central aisle followed a little way behind by her servant bearing a footwarmer, to keep Madame's feet warm during the service.

So there were a few colourful details in the greyness of my first year at Capestang. And, in spite of it all, I found a ray of sunshine in the company of the Thouret family. Delightfully bohemian and unconforming, as happy-go-lucky as crickets, their home was a special place where I forgot the bitterness of my disappointments. Monsieur Thouret, a short man, with a very open expression, was secretary to the *mairie* and had the post of conductor to the municipal orchestra; Emile was the assistant conductor, and they both had a great respect for each other, strengthened by their common interest. Madame Thouret, a violinist and daughter of a conductor, didn't take her domestic tasks too seriously and was more at ease with a bow in her hand. Juliette and Pierrette, their two daughters, were both artistically gifted. The elder taught elocution at the Toulouse conservatoire and her sister became a great per-former of realist songs. Under this roof, malicious gossip and envy had no place, songs and laughter mingled constantly, and we found ourselves entirely in accord with this happy, healthy atmosphere.

The years have passed ... the house has changed hands several times, and I feel nostalgic when I recall the even-ing when, in front of its modest front door, my husband conducted a serenade for Juliette's wedding, and the splendid day when there was great excitement in the big room of the house to welcome the orchestra from Paris in which Pierrette was singing.

The municipality recognised our friend's value when the road in which one side of our house stood was called Gaston Thouret. An honour which he deserved.

I was amazed at the wealth of nicknames by which the village inhabitants were known. Some of them had to do with a physical characteristic:

Pel roge: red hair
Plançon: young tree (a short person)
Closco d'oliva: an olive (referring to the shape of the head)
L'empesat: starched (stiffly dressed)

Others denoted a profession or hobby:

La repetito: fishmonger
Copa campanas: bell-ringer
L'alumetaire: match-seller

Or noted a particular taste for something:

Castanha: for chestnuts
Ventresca: for pork fat

and others were more colourful or more Gallic:

L'Esquina canda: warm back
'lou pissarel': john willy
'lou cuol de férre': hot pants (of easy virtue)

I have a long list of them, and some of them still remain, others have been lost and the people who would have been able to enlighten me about their origins have gone too.

'When an old person dies, a reference library closes.' This is why I am trying to collect and save these rural treasures.

After a year of working at the primary school, I was transferred to the infant school at my request, and was thrilled to be back with the youngest children again – at a stage which I particularly enjoyed teaching – and in a relaxed atmosphere with delightful colleagues.

The premises were dilapidated and inconvenient, but the atmosphere was friendly, and I spent some wonderfully happy years there. There was great trust between us, and we would hurry to meet up with one another to exchange anecdotes of our little domestic upsets. For various reasons I had to teach in all three divisions, but my longest stint was with the 'babies', virgin wax which needs to be shaped carefully. Teaching them was a task to which I was devoted, and it felt like an act of love: I always respected the children greatly, and was careful not to hurt such delicate sensitivity. I realised that it demanded my all. A child has need of sound judgement, quickly tires of things which are too easy, and prefers to be asked to make an effort which brings it joy in success. As a teacher to children, one has unrivalled influence and from them, complete support. I owe to them my youthful spirit and enthusiasm which I still have today.

Outside school hours I worked hard making sensory games and teaching material, as in those days we did not have the ever more enticing range of articles that are available to the teachers of today. As I enjoyed occasions for celebration, I coerced my colleagues into organising entertainments which involved us in extra work.

For his part, Emile was very busy; in the mornings he worked in the vines, to which he was hardly suited; in the afternoons, he taught music and singing in all classes from the infant school to the college, which meant that he was involved in all school functions; before supper he gave individual lessons, and his evenings were spent in a hall in the *mairie* where he got together the children of the commune for classes in theory and playing of instruments, alternating with rehearsals of the town band. He had taken on the post of their conductor and was passionately devoted to it. Making good use of the enlightened counsel of his predecessor, he led the 46 players of the Lyre Capestanaise to triumph at the festival competition in Castres in 1947, and Bédarieux in 1949. With his musicians, he organised theatre evenings which were well supported by the public, who were not yet in the grip of television.

But he saved his most impressive work for the Carnival: he composed polished, very amusing musical interludes which his team, made up of tough members of the rugby team, found very satisfying. The Carnival was a highlight for the village, where it was celebrated with gusto.

After being carried away by the attractions of the fairground, the revellers used to crowd into the dance hall, abandoning themselves to wild dances and *farandoles*: the various disguises fascinated the onlookers who would guffaw at the ridiculous antics of the groups dressed in drag. The long-awaited moment for the presentation of the sketch by Bélet and his Boys came in the middle of the evening. There would be a different theme each day; here are a few of them:

'Le ballet des petits rats de l'Opéra' – a few skits from the television: 'La descente de Nounours et du marchand de sable', 'L'envahissement de l'étang par Allaryx le Gaulois' (the hero of which was a local rugbyman) – and even a few attacks on the negligence of the town council: 'Le ballet des seaux' mimed the daily collection of the night soil buckets in the village streets ... These sketches had taken many hilarious winter evenings of preparation, laughter and fun, dedicated to making the costumes and rehearsing the script. Thus the artistic life that the village had known for decades was able to continue through such events.

These many activities were not very lucrative: the sale of wine scarcely brought in anything and was barely enough to cater for the needs of his family; his job with the municipality was poorly paid and his lessons were given for a very modest fee – some of them even free!

He loved creating things, and I suspect he often abandoned the mattock or the copper-sulphate spraying machine, to compose a poem in the shelter of a hillock. He was an artist and we all adored him. The stage was the best place for him to give full rein to his natural talents. He had several strings to his bow! Equally happy playing the violin or the saxophone, he also had outstanding diction, and was just as successful acting in tragedy as in comedy. Tired of interpreting the work of others, he threw himself into writing pithy songs, thus satisfying his taste for satire, preferring to express himself in the Occitan language which he loved for its rich texture.

E de la boca a l'aurelha
Los qu'apelan lengas de pelha
Plantadas coma lo piquet
L'er finot, plenas de caquet
Pelan lo vesin, la vesina
Memes lo fraire o la cosina
E se quauqu'una manca un jorn
Es sovent pelada a son torn.

(And from mouth to ear,
Whispering with tongues of chiffon,
They stand there planted like poles,
With wily air, full of biting eloquence
They speak ill of a neighbour or a neighbour's wife,
Even of a brother, or a cousin,
And if one of them is not there one day,
She is torn apart in her turn.)

He took part in many literary competitions and brought back flattering awards; Aubanel published his sketch 'Le Noël du vagabond'. Musician, composer, actor, writer, singer, specialist in the *langue d'oc*, he reserved all his talents for his village, to which he gave freely of his sparkle all his life long.

The young people of the Foyer Rural highly valued his place in local heritage and took the initiative of collecting some of his works in a book for sale to the public, a tribute which was one of his last joys.

'Pourquoi ne pas louer les gens de bien de leur vivant puisqu'ils n'entendent rien sous la tombe?' (Diderot) (Why not praise good men while they are living, for they hear nothing in the grave?)

Thank you, young people!

In 1936, a great hope was born in France: the formation of the popular front, prelude to a social revolution which would improve the workers' lot: the 40-hour week and the first paid holidays received a frenzied welcome. I bitterly regretted that my father did not see the fruition of what he had always worked and hoped for.

In the privacy of our marriage, we longed to have a child, and the news that it was on the way was welcomed with excitement; our hope was called Remi right through my pregnancy, and indeed it was he who came into the world on 7th January 1937 at 5.0 p.m. after a long and difficult birth.

On the evening of the 6th, I had started my labour, and the midwife was at my side, wrapped in a large shawl. In those days births took place in the mother's home and the whole house was in a state of commotion. Alcohol was burned in a receptacle from time to time to increase the warmth of the room. As chance would have it, a play was being put on that evening, and the presence of Emile in his roles of stage manager, musician and actor, was indispensable. He was in quite a nervous state behind the scenes, bumping into everyone, and often coming to the house for news in his stage costume. Luckily we lived not far from the village hall. He did not want to miss the arrival of the baby: but this was so long in happening, that at the long awaited moment, Emile was fast asleep downstairs, exhausted by a very disturbed and sleepless night.

It seems simplistic to recount the wonderment of the arrival of our first child, and to recall our ecstasy in examining his little body from head to toe. On these occasions we are filled with pride as if we were the only people in the world to delight in the miracle of creation. From that moment on, our lives are enriched with a potential for love and hope.

Remi grew into a lovely child, and I was very proud of my little boy with his pink face lit with blue eyes under fair curly hair. He adored snuggling up in the arms of his Daddy who cuddled him in his moments of relaxation.

The war, however, came to shatter this happiness...

XVI

It came to catch us unawares right in the middle of our holidays: as I was subject to frequent and painful bilious attacks, I agreed to start a cure at Vichy in August 1939. We were staying at a simple guest house so that we could save some of our money to go to the magnificent concerts which this then booming spa town had to offer; our little Remi discovered new amusements in the varied play equipment in the children's park and enjoyed the pony rides.

There were evening performances of opera at the Casino, but the price of the tickets was very high: there were only two suitable places that were inexpensive; so one had to be first or second in the queue which started forming at 6.0 a.m. for a three-hour wait – the box office opened at 9. Emile undertook this chore several times, so that we could enjoy a good production in turns; looking after Remi made it impossible for us to go out together.

At the end of our stay, Emile wanted to go and pay a surprise visit to a friend with whom he had been during the German occupation in 1927, and who lived at Saint Pourçain sur Sioule, 28 kilometres from Vichy. We received a very warm welcome, and forged the bonds of a great friendship which still exists today. We would have prolonged our stay in this very hospitable home, but alarming news was circulating – the peace was threatened...

We returned hurriedly to Vichy in a very crowded train, managing to squeeze ourselves into the vestibule of the carriage.

On 2nd September we got up very early and returned home, delighted with the splendid crop of *azerolles* which we had gathered in the countryside to make into delicious jellies.

An unusual activity reigned in the village, the walls covered with posters: 'La mobilisation Générale!' (General call-up!) We were dumbfounded – we were hoping for a miracle after the Munich agreement – but we had not realised the betrayal.

Emile was conscripted into the 255th regiment at Vallauris on the Côte d'Azur: this was a tremendous stroke of luck for him. Jo Bouillon was enlisted in this regiment, and had the idea of forming a military jazz band (to keep up the morale on the home front) and organising benevolent concerts.

Although he had no diplomas, my husband was enrolled in this band with 18 others, some of whom had won first prizes from conservatoires. Thus, for him, war time was a period when he was privileged to have the pleasure of giving himself to his music in the company of top class musicians. Sometimes he sat at the violin desk, and sometimes with the saxophones. He was also much appreciated in comic items, particularly in his impersonations of Fernandel: 'Bélet was an exciting comedian' was the comment in a report of a concert at Golfe Juan in January 1940.

The comfort of his situation and the proximity of the area meant that I could go and visit him, first during the Christmas holidays, when we saw the branches of mimosa sagging under the weight of the snow; we ensconced ourselves in an isolated villa, with no heating, but we were together. At Pentecost, as Emile got on well with his superiors, he installed me in a comfortable hotel. Apart from the joy of being together again, we loved discovering the attractions of this beautiful region. My stay was cut short by Italy coming into the war on 10th June; it was unwise to stay in a military operational zone. We listened in to the news on the radio, which was not reassuring, and became less so each hour, sounding the knell of our wonderful holiday. So I left, feeling very anxious for the future, but enriched with wonderful memories.

On 22nd June, the armistice was signed. If Emile had been fortunate during this war, there were other, tragic situations, and some very painful experiences, such as those of my cousin Jean; the declaration of war had come upon him after long months of military service; the leave he had hoped for was suspended, and he had to go off to the front line without having had the comfort of seeing his family. He knew my optimism, and he wrote to me: 'I count on you, Marthe, to comfort me with your letters which give me so much courage. Our lieutenant said to us: "The Germans have occupied Arras and Amiens. An urgent task is ahead of you; if you do not want your wives, mothers or sisters to become Germans one day, I think you will do your utmost to defend your country."'

And my young cousin, 20 years old, overcome by this speech, and full of good sense, ended: 'His words are splendid, but for those whom we love, it would be much better to stay alive!'

In the village, deprived of able-bodied men, life organised itself as well as could be expected. I, personally, was fortunate to have a profession which kept the wolf from my door, gave me pleasant and comforting contact with my colleagues and the children who communicated their lack of concern and their joy of life to me. Remi, who was now old enough to go to school, shared my routine, which made life easier. In other respects, I was hard put to cope with the few vines that we possessed; labour was scarce, and many were the Thursdays when I exchanged the pen for the pickaxe which I wielded very clumsily. That year the *vendanges* took place half-heartedly, and with difficulties; the *saquettes* were meagre. We knew what it was to go hungry, and we were happy to eat as many grapes as we could. I discovered that the Lézignan onion had a particularly good flavour, and I took one every day in my *colle*; with a nice aramon grape this calmed our appetites, made keener in the fresh country air.

In our daily round, everyone's concern was to feed themselves and to keep warm. Each citizen had a *carte d'alimentation*, which differed according to age, to enable us to buy provisions (bread, milk, meat, cheese, and fats), or household necessities such as coal, soap, cloth, shoes, and even tobacco. These cards were made up of tickets which had to be handed over to the retailers. The portions allocated were very meagre (275 g of bread a day for those aged 21 to 70), and we were always looking for ways to increase them; we used to bicycle into the neighbouring Aude, where some tickets were better credited.

During the holidays, we used to go from Saint-Thibéry to Bessan, to buy, after several hours' wait, sausage made from donkey meat, which was on unrestricted sale.

The worst thing was the scarcity of bread; the allocated round loaf was of poor quality, very dense and yellow, because it was often filled up with maize flour. Consequently, I am outraged these days, when I see the good bread that we missed so much, thrown away in the dustbins!

This penury caused the black market to hold sway; it brought comfortable profits to the smart and unscrupulous traders who went to stock up in the more favoured regions and secretly sold their wares at very high prices.

Green vegetables and fruit were not distributed by quotas. When a sale of them was announced by the town crier, we rushed to line up in a long queue, and it often happened that the long-awaited baskets were emptied before our turn came. Everyone's dream was to have garden: so when Emile came back, we bought a little villa which had the advantage of being surrounded by a plot of land with a well on it. We had to work the pump for ages to do the watering, but the produce improved our diet.

There we were able to breed rabbits and have a hen house which meant we could eat real eggs – much better than the yellow powder which was sold to us. When he discovered that there was a goat-breeder at Sigéan, Emile went there with a friend on a tandem pulling a trailer. The animals were not securely tied, and escaped into the countryside on the way home. They were capricious and swift creatures and it was not easy to recapture them running through the vines. But our men put their all into doing so, as it was a promise of milk and kids. Our Grisette gave us two. We introduced new vegetables into our diet: swedes, Jerusalem artichokes, and *vesces* which we served first to the animals. Once I made a meal of dried haricots, their weevils removed with a needle, and I cooked fresh peas in their pods with the thin skin removed. *Pâtés* of figs were our party sweetmeats, and we made great cauldrons of *raisiné* (made by cooking the grape seeds) for our desserts.

At the school they tried to rectify the deficiencies in the children's diet by regular distributions of milk, jam, rice pudding and vitamin biscuits. The older children were even supplied with cooked dishes, which were greatly appreciated by the pupils.

The wine-growers got themselves organised to provide themselves with food. They had *correspondants* in the mountains (in the Lozère, Aveyron and Cantal) with whom to exchange their wine for the commodities of which we were deprived. They had to go by train and seek them out on the spot; part of the trip was sometimes made on foot in difficult circumstances, but they were delighted to bring home the wherewithal to feed acceptably for several weeks. These journeys were dangerous, as the watch on economic control was very strict, and sometimes the hardly gained provisions were seized, or subjected to a heavy fine. Emile did not want to do it; our stomachs were not very demanding, and we were able to satisfy Remi's hunger, as he was only four. One time only he risked going to our friends in the Allier who offered us half a pig. Coming back, the suitcase gave way and spilled part of the contents onto the platform at Béziers station; he got such a fright that he never did it again!

We ran short of absolutely everything; but need makes for ingenuity: we made a substitute for soap with perborate of soda: we cut soles out of old tyres, around which we sewed thick cloth, to make slippers. Wool from old knitted garments and cotton from baby wrappers was re-cycled. A craftsman made me some clogs in raffia lined with rabbit skin; they weren't elegant, but they were comfortable for we suffered from the cold. The streets resounded with the clatter of wooden soles which all the women had taken to wearing.

The smokers were *en manque*: they rolled their cigarettes, or filled their pipes with the remains of fodder or other substitutes. One mother of a large family confided to me, in tears, that her husband had bartered a doe rabbit which was about to give birth, for a few packets of tobacco!

Entertainments were few and far between; but relationships between neighbours were closer; we helped one another out, and we exchanged a lot of correspondence: apart from the daily letter to those who were absent, there were the messages of comfort to those who suffered from the present situation: to Margot, so anguished by the lack of news from her husband and eventually 'reassured' when she learnt he was a prisoner, and to our

141

friend from Saint Pourçain, bravely taking care of her family and looking after the business during Marcel's captivity.

All these prisoners of war dreamed of their escapes, and some of them were perilous, such as the one my friend Lucille's husband told me about:

We were four pals who decided to 'go for it'. Our plan was to get into a wine tanker going to France. We got provisions together, water, minimum washing things and a large receptacle for our bodily functions. It was this that gave us the most trouble; at each jolt it had to be held securely and we had to impose strict discipline on ourselves not to overfill it. We were in a very uncomfortable position; a dim light filtered in through the wooden slats; often we were thrown off balance; the noise of the movement was almost deafening, but each turn of the wheel was bringing us closer to freedom. Since I came back, my sleep is peopled with nightmares, and I struggle in a circle which goes endlessly round and round.

* * *

Capestang's population altered with the mass arrival of refugees. They came in pitiful hordes, crammed into trains, makeshift cars which crawled along the roads, old men, women and children from the north and east of France, to invade the Midi – a free zone!

The watchwords became sacrifice and dedication, and there was no lack of occasion to observe them.

In May 1940, the Belgians arrived with us: we had given hospitality in our house at Saint-Thibéry to the Husquinet family from Liège: there they found comfort and pleasant surroundings. Blanche, who was the head of the family, came back afterwards each year to stay with us until she died.

Some of their compatriots came to occupy houses next to ours in Capestang, and they spoke with emotion of all they had had to leave behind in such haste.

We gave them practical and spiritual help and support, and bonds were forged which still exist. There were often alarms during the day time, and at the wail of the siren, we gathered a few precious belongings in a bag and the whole neighbourhood went in the direction of the *étang*.

The children used to enjoy this diversion; under the trees in the countryside and in the maize fields, they organised quiet games and were sorry when the alert ended and brought them back to normal life.

At the infant school, an opening had been made in the wall to allow access into the grounds next door, where trenches had been dug out in case of air attacks during school hours. The primary school children were put through exercises in the course of which alarms were simulated; they were then asked to take shelter under their school desks, and woe betide the bottoms that protruded!

The school day began with the saluting of the colours: the French flag was hoisted to the top of a mast, while the assembled children sang:

> Maréchal, nous voilà!
> Devant toi, le sauveur de la France,
> Nous jurons, nous tes gars
> De servir et de suivre tes pas.
> Maréchal, nous voilà,
> Tu nous a redonné l'espérance
> La Patrie renaîtra
> Maréchal, nous voilà

> (Marshal, here we are!
> Before you, saviour of France,
> We your children, promise
> To serve you and follow in your footsteps.
> Marshal, here we are!
> You have given us back our hope
> The fatherland will be reborn
> Marshal, here we are!)

At that particular time, there was a dedicated cult surrounding the hero of Verdun who was immensely popular. But the French were cold and hungry, and the penury, added to the collaboration with the enemy which was affirmed by the

Vichy government, swayed the opinion of the country to break away progressively from the Marshal's regime.

When, after the decision of the presiding government to sign the Armistice, the rousing appeal by General de Gaulle rang out from BBC London on 18th June 1940 ('I invite all French people, wherever they may be, to join me in battle, in sacrifice and in hope. Our country is in danger of death. Let us all struggle to save her.'), a patriotic fervour seized the French population. The price that they would have to pay for the end of the conflict was incompatible with the honour and dignity of France: – occupation of Paris, and of more than a half of the territory,

– the loss of Alsace and Lorraine,

– food rationing: abolition of human rights,

– deposition of many elected mayors,

– suspension of parliament; antisemitic and antimasonic laws; redundancy of republican *fonctionnaires* etc.,...

In the face of these humiliating conditions, reserves of voluntary resistance formed, and their plan of action was guided by London radio: 'This is London calling. This is the French speaking to the French.'

These broadcasts, giving precise information on what was happening, were listened to religiously in many homes. The press and French radio were under German control, and gave false news. From London, we were able to hear the voice of Jean Oberlé, the 'street urchin' of Paris, who used to hum to the tune of the Quintonine: 'Radio Paris ment; Radio Paris est allemand.' (Radio Paris is lying; Radio Paris is German.)

In our house we turned down the volume and listened with our ears close to the receiver, for under cover of darkness, the village collaborators crept up to houses to betray those who were sustained by this voice from across the Channel.

* * *

Our task was to do something for the prisoners of war; my husband thought of putting on a large-scale production for their benefit, which would draw a large audience and make our compatriots forget, momentarily, their material anxieties and gloom. I longed to do *L'Arlésienne* by Daudet, made so rich by Bizet's beautiful score: although it was very ambitious, this choice was accepted. The people of Capestang had been well practised in the theatre arts through the auspices of their three dramatic societies, 'Les Amusaires,' 'L'Aurore artistique et littéraire' and 'Le Cercle'. Emile was persuaded to find the means of staging this Provençal drama. The parts were allotted, and a marvellous experience began; but ... the Germans, breaking the Armistice conditions, occupied our region from 1st November 1942, in reply to the Allied landings in North Africa. We were submitted to severe restrictions. There was a curfew which had to be observed, and we had to endure numerous electricity cuts; so we often rehearsed in the dim light of a miner's lamp. Two escorts, picked by the occupying army and armed with passes, were obliged to accompany home all the members of their group right to their doorsteps; the anxiety was acute when they met a German patrol, for Monsieur Lejbowicz, of Jewish descent, was amongst us in the role of stage manager.

As the Capestang town orchestra did not have enough instruments for the Bizet score, a society from Béziers, 'Les Amis de la Musique', made up the missing musical parts. This group often had to travel to coordinate the text and the music, and we had to make sacrifices for their transport, and some-times their refreshment, in times of hardship. Choudens' publishing company had demanded a large bond in return for lending us the one and only copy of the integral work, and, in these troubled times we were uncertain of recuperating our financial outlay.

All these difficulties, added to local scepticism which showed itself in mocking remarks, galvanised the troupe, and gave it a spirit which helped to overcome all the obstacles. After three months of rehearsals, we gave two performances to full houses in Capestang. The part of Rose, which had been given to me, suited my passionate nature to perfection, and I entered into it with great fervour. Through this venture I experienced the agonies and joys of being an actress: the hollow feeling in the pit of the stomach before going on stage, the terror of 'drying up', and the heady thrill of success, that electricity which communicates with the audience and draws forth strengths in oneself which one had no idea existed.

'Et puis, il y a la joie de faire partie d'un groupe, de s'y

145

fondre sans s'y perdre, d'y être responsable sans s'y trouver seul, d'être épaulé et soutenu comme on épaule et soutient les autres.' (And then there is the joy of being part of a group, of merging in it without losing one's identity, of being responsible without being alone, of being supported and sustained, as one supports and sustains others.)

We all had to congratulate our accompanists. In this work, the musical support had had a transcendent effect on our performance. Ever since, hearing this beautiful music arouses in me deep feeling and nostalgia. It was a great success, evident from the offer to put on our show in Béziers municipal theatre: this performance took place in May 1944 on the Thursday of Ascension: the auditorium was well filled, despite the threat of round-ups which were regularly carried out on the occasion of a show; the seats in front of the orchestra stalls were filled with German officers. We felt the audience thrill, and a press review is proof of it:

That mere amateurs could risk producing on a Béziers stage the immortal Provençal drama by that prince of French storytellers, Alphonse Daudet, might have seemed an impertinence, when one thinks of the great artists of the Comédie Française whom all 'Bittérois' have seen parading on the vast stage of the Arènes. And, moreover, playing for the benefit of the prisoners of war, a group of amateurs brilliantly achieved the impossible, and the heartfelt ripple of applause which broke out from all parts of the theatre was the most eloquent testimony of this ... They gave the audience the opportunity to reward the very high artistic standard of the production.

Encouraged by this marvellous outcome, we would certainly have organised a tour in the region, but a few days afterwards, disaster struck the village.

XVII

The 6th June 1944, the day of the Normandy landings, was a day of glory and was full of hope for France. With us, it was a day of intense and feverish activity which had tragic consequences.

The previous evening, London radio had broadcast the code phrase to signal the departure of our resistants for the Maquis of Captain La Tourette, in the foothills of L'Espinouse, to the north of Saint-Chinian. The preparations were indiscreet; certain people involved went through the streets of the village armed with sub-machine guns ... The news was whispered round: 'The departure is this evening' – unwise revelations of a manoeuvre which had to be kept secret.

Next day, 7th June, in the early hours of the morning, consternation reigned in the village: the lorries carrying our men had been intercepted by the German forces in the narrow pass of the Col de Fontjun, a perfect place strategically, a bottleneck in the road, flanked by high, steep escarpments, so ideal for an ambush that it is certain that the surprise attack had been meticulously prepared – and as the result of what information?

The question remains unanswered to this day.

There was bitter fighting, and the forces were unequal: the lorries exploded; some of the occupants, including the local leader, suffered a horrible death; some resistants were killed on the spot; others, under the cover of the darkness, tried by climbing and running wildly through the vines to escape the hail of bullets. Some of them took refuge in the *cabanots*, basic constructions used by the wine-growers; they stayed hidden there during the whole Occupation and were looked after and fed (some of them were severely wounded) by brave and generous fellow countrymen ... But 18 of them, who made up the whole section around Capestang, were captured and taken to Béziers to the Du Guesclin barracks. The following day, lined up against the wall in a pitiful state, after terrible tortures, their arms tied to the balustrade above their heads, they were faced by the firing squad. Sadistically, the German executioners forced the passers-by to witness this slaughter. From the breast of one young man burst forth the desperate cry of every man seeking the supreme refuge in adversity: 'Maman!'

The only woman of the convoy, having watched her husband fall down under the bullets, and faced with the army aiming at her, bravely cried out: 'Vive la France!', and in a few minutes their little boy was an orphan: 18 shots shattered the serenity of that fine June afternoon before a terrorised public, who contained its disgust and hatred. Champs de Mars square is stamped for ever with this blind atrocity of the war.

Many of Capestang's children, having had faith in their involvement in the service of their country, were cut down in the prime of youth. Ever since, 7th June reverberates sorrowfully in the hearts of the contemporaries of this tragedy: each year the memory of the victims is honoured, and street plaques in the village remind us of their sacrifice, but nothing can diminish the grief of their families and friends.

The reprisals were not long in coming: on 9th June, Capestang was surrounded by German lorries, the town square overrun with tanks, and in the afternoon the loudspeaker from the *mairie* broadcast this terrible order:

'All men between the ages of 18 and 40 must come to the Place Jean Jaurès with a kit bag.'

(By negotiating, the mayor had managed to reduce the number, which was originally all between the ages of 18 and 60 years.)

This call reached me in the school playground. That day, my husband had been drafted for compulsory service, drilling holes in the road to Carcassonne. I packed some provisions and a few of his possessions in a rucksack. Swift and heartbreaking farewells followed. With Emile gone, we were three women left in anguish: my handicapped mother, my asthmatic mother-in-law, a seven-year-old child, and myself gathering my courage to support my little family ... A few moments later a German officer and two soldiers invaded the house for a search: all the furniture was gone through, the drawers emptied, and the tiles of the attic thrust up with the butts of rifles to detect hidden arms.

We were watching this devastation without moving when the officer beckoned me to follow him into the bedroom. The intervention of my mother-in-law, rightly anxious at this request, saved me a terrible experience ... The repulsive man came and threatened me with his gun to overcome my resistance: when he was interrupted he uttered cries of rage, and then a soldier presented him with a letter which seemed to fill him with joy; he dragged my mother-in-law off to the *mairie* between two sub-machine guns, and as she crossed the square, where Emile was held with 200 men, that was the last sight that he had of his mother before he left.

Amongst them was one of Emile's cousins from Agde, who fearing a landing in that town had asked his family for hospitality. It was the wish of fate that, fleeing from a possible threat, he suffered the unhappy lot of our townsmen.

They were there in groups, anxious but resolute, surrounded by the German army who were joined by the 'collabos'. These played an active part, pointing out their friends who were immediately set free from the ranks: my husband was not amongst them, but one of them said to him 'generously':

'Emile, you have done too much for the village; you will not have your name put forward as a resistant.'

The sad cohort, reduced to 185 men, started to walk towards Béziers, casting a last look at the church tower, which they had just saved by their surrender.

During this time, my mother-in-law, at the *mairie*, had met up with people who had had compromising documents or arms discovered in their homes.

We wondered anxiously what could be the contents of the intercepted letter which was amongst Emile's personal papers. The explanation was as follows: At the time *L'Arlésienne* was being produced, the part of the herdsman was played by a man from Lorraine who was living in Capestang; in the play,

149

he had to deliver a letter to Frederic, who was played by my husband. It was just one letter, written for this particular occasion, and could have been read by anyone. It was this that Emile had rashly tidied away amongst his papers ... seeing that it had been sent from a town in Lorraine, the German soldier had thought it was suspicious.

Luckily it contained nothing subversive against the Germans and my mother-in-law was allowed to go free ... but it could have been otherwise! The ways of destiny are uncertain!

Our men from Capestang were shut up in the du Guesclin barracks in Béziers, the recent setting of the appalling massacre.

In the village, far from binding the inhabitants together, the terrible ordeals set them against one another, and malicious gossip thrived. Through our professional and social doings, we played a little part in the life of the community: I think it was because of this that we were set against as a couple: Emile was accused of coercing the young people to join the resistance; some people even maintained that the rehearsals for *L'Arlésienne* were a pretext for spreading propaganda. So it was an easy step from there to deduce that it was he who was responsible for their deaths. These were serious allegations. The accusation gave me the boldness to go by bicycle through the vines (we were forbidden to use the roads), to try and have an interview, perhaps the last one, with my husband. I had the assurance that he was innocent of these accusations, and I was heartened to observe the warm friendship with which his comrades surrounded him, gaining from his wisdom and optimism on many occasions.

On my return to Capestang, the curfew had already fallen; I was accosted by a German patrol and escorted to my house after being admonished in no uncertain terms. But I was pleased with the step I had taken, the more so when our men left Béziers the night following my visit.

The news of the disasters at Capestang spread through the country, and spontaneously from Saint Pourçain, Frontignan and Saint-Thibéry, shelter was offered to Emile to spare him from being deported. Although this help was useless, I felt very grateful to these true friends, who did not hesitate to run risks for our security.

Capestang was then living completely under the German

heel. The commandant installed himself in a bourgeois house, and it became the administrative headquarters of the village. The school life was turned upside down: primary schools and colleges were emptied of all their occupants; teaching took place in empty houses little adapted to the children's needs, with no playground nor WC. The teachers were re-housed in unoccupied buildings. The boys' school was turned into a hospital where the wounded German soldiers were nursed. The German authorities ran the local life; it was necessary to have a pass issued by them in order to move outside the village limits, and cars and horses were requisitioned.

The occupying army had access to the inside of houses, no doors were to be locked, even at night.

In the silence of the sleeping town, which came early because of the curfew, one heard the sound of boots ringing on the cobblestones, and when we heard them stop outside our house we trembled with fear. We were only women and children at home! Each evening, my mother, who was haunted by my attempted rape by the German officer, made me drag the furniture against the door of the bedroom I shared with Remi.

We lived in continuous bondage, and not knowing what fate had befallen our men who had been taken away from us ... They had left Béziers on 13th June ... not one of them had tried to escape for fear of compromising the fate of his comrades. Later we learned that they had made a halt in the east, in the uncomfortable camp of Soest, before being sent to Germany; that country was then exhausted by the war and lacked a labour force; this situation saved our Capestang men from the death camps. Only Monsieur Lejbowicz, of Jewish descent, was sent to Auschwitz.

Our men were treated like slaves or animals; they were lined up, had their muscles felt, their strength and resistance evaluated; some bosses fought amongst one another for the most robust: a large number joined the factories at Bochum, the rest were dispersed amongst the farms. Emile was one of these, and found himself on a large landed property at Laasphe in Westphalia. He was put in charge of the livestock which was made up mostly of cattle, about which he knew nothing, and of the cultivation of the fields, which were reserved above all for growing potatoes; this vegetable made up the major part of the diet, and would have been enough to stay his hunger if he had been able to eat it; but as soon as he began his meal, the boss ordered him to get back to work. Through this he lost 15 kilos in a month, suffered from dysentery and fed himself on green apples gleaned in the fields. Treated roughly, called 'terrorist' by his employers who were all dedicated to the Führer, and suffering from starvation, he decided to get himself sacked as he felt he could not stand up to such treatment: he made a mess of the work, and having a smattering of the German language from the Occupation of 1927, he shouted abuse at the daughters of the family, who belonged to Hitler's Youth, threatening that he would denounce them to the Americans after the liberation which would not be long in coming.

A few days later he was collected and taken to a dairy, where he was given the job of distributing milk churns in the surrounding area, in the company of prisoners. There was an incident in which he was badly gassed in the lorry in a serious road accident, but the atmosphere was quite different to that on the farm. He was permanently in touch with the French prisoners in a camp nearby; he used to 'feast' with them on Sundays on the 'sumptuous' banquet of cat and fox stew, rounded off with the cream that he regularly skimmed off the milk. He was able to go and visit some other men from Capestang who were isolated on farms, to give them a bit of cheer and talk of home.

All these bits of news came to us via cards, which, after a month of anxious silence, we began to receive fairly regularly.

Once we knew where our absent menfolk were, we were able to add to our information and share news with the families of those who were in the same region. We pulled together to try and give practical help to those who were most in need, and formed an association. The president was Madame Bonnafous, the mother of a large family, who had had the immense grief of seeing three of her sons, handsome boys in the prime of youth, depart on 9th June. I was put on the committee; Madame Bonnafous, who was not used to public speaking, nor writing, always made me speak at the meetings and begged me to write the letters ... but her level-headedness and experience were invaluable to us.

From June 1944 until May 1945, was a time of intense activity for me, what with my family, the school, and so many individual homes to support. Many women, confined to their domestic role, had never been involved in administrative tasks, leaving these to their husbands. A stream of these followed during my free time, and I became a sort of 'public scribe'. Listening to these other women, who sometimes revealed dreadful situations, made me forget my own troubles, and stopped me from sinking into despondency. Nevertheless, things did not always go smoothly, and the meetings were often stormy. I remember the general outcry when an explanation was asked for about the tax exemptions, which favoured certain families according to their particular circumstances; even though the committee had discussed this at length, and in all possible fairness with the inspector, man is nevertheless sensitive where his purse is concerned!

We also tried to amalgamate with the association of prisoners' families, which was smaller than ours, but more experienced. In spite of the good will, this was a failure, each camp declaring itself more proven than the other.

Despite the re-found trust of my fellow countrywomen, I had not forgotten the accusation against Emile, and I was anxious to bring it out into the open. I had an opportunity to do so on the evening of 21st November 1944, when a large part of the village had gathered together in the Maison du Peuple, for the business of an illicit distribution of provisions to selected people. The scandalous goings-on attracted a crowd. I took advantage of this to get up on the stage and restore my husband's good name, recalling the exact facts and calling on numerous witnesses. I had the gratification of frequent applause, and many hands were extended when I had finished by urging the population of Capestang to pull together in harmony.

From outside, various news reached us: the appalling massacre at Oradour sur Glane sounded a particularly grim echo for Capestang, which would have suffered the same fate had it not been for the brave intervention of our mayor and the disciplined bearing of the inhabitants. On 15th August

153

1944, the announcement of the landings of the southern armies at Dramont in Provence under the command of General De Lattre de Tassigny, filled us with hope. Ten days later, Paris was liberated! 'An immense joy, a powerful pride, has unfurled over the nation. And more ... the whole world trembled when it knew that Paris had emerged from the abyss and that its light would shine again.'

General de Gaulle's speech communicated a euphoria to us that was fleeting – for us, the Germans were still there, and for long months ahead, we still had to shoulder the role of heads of the family.

We organised our lives within the limits of what was available locally: trips to the seaside were out, so we took the children to bathe in the canal, the water of which was clean as there was no traffic on it. It was a life without joy, and always with some new complication.

The few relatives who had escaped being deported, benefiting from privileged circumstances, had left me to struggle in my difficulties, particularly those concerning the upkeep of the vines, and sometimes even refused their help. I have forgiven them, but I have not forgotten. I particularly remember a very dangerous descent I had to make with a handcart loaded with the pickings, mercifully very meagre, from a vine located high up on the 'Louiset', as I had found no one to transport it for me.

We do not always stick together in adversity!

XVIII

On 12th May 1945, I was informed of my husband's return; a neighbour and friend who had shared help and support during this difficult time received the same happy news simultaneously. What a beautiful day was that Friday 13th!

We mobilised a shopkeeper's van; with hearts aglow we rediscovered an interest in our appearance; we dressed carefully and set off with wild enthusiasm to meet our homecomers.

There was great bustle at Béziers station, moving reunions punctuated with laughter and tears, boisterous embraces, anxious faces, ill-assorted garments ... We presented ourselves at the reception desk and were directed towards the appointed platform.

At last, the train arrives ... my heart is thumping very strongly. This joy is unbearable. We look at all the arrivals, and with equal fervour we run towards two men who look like tramps, strangely kitted out, against whom we cuddle up with all the love accumulated over ten long months. Emile is wearing a dreadful old felt hat, and a long, worn greatcoat. The arch of his eyebrow is open, the result of the aggression of a German who had thrown a can of milk at his head.

Badly shaved, very tired, our husbands were scarcely triumphant. We felt almost ashamed of our jubilation.

A liberated compatriot, having nothing but a guitar for his luggage, joined us in the van. At the Trézilles bridge, strong emotions overcame them at the sight of their church tower which they had feared never to see again. Many people called to visit at our home; everyone wanted to know how the repatriation had taken place.

We had to reassure the wife of one of Emile's companions

who had not been amongst the same convoy: 'Don't be afraid to tell me the truth,' she moaned. 'Don't distress yourself so! I promise you he will be here in eight days.' We could not tell her that he wanted more time to celebrate his good luck!

They had been liberated by the Americans and sent into Belgium where they were given a very warm welcome. As my husband was passing a bookshop, the shopkeeper gave him a beautiful book, saying to him: 'I have put a bookmark inside.' It was a bank note! It was very different in Paris, where people avoided them with some mistrust. It is true that they were scarcely attractive to look at!

He told me of some moving moments; of how, defying his gaolers on 14th July, he sang a ringing Marseillaise at the top of his voice: and true to his passion for expressing his sorrows and desires in song, he composed 'The Song of Return', rich with his experiences:

Refrain:

> Le plus beau jour de ma vie
> Sera celui du retour,
> Quittant alors Westphalie
> Je reviendrai pour toujours.
> Beau jour attendu sans cesse
> Pour moi tu seras rempli d'allégresse,
> Le plus beau jour de ma vie
> Sera celui du retour.
>
> J'attends la fin de nos misères
> Avec patience et fierté,
> Car je sais que sur cette terre
> Nous reviendra la liberté,
> Et malgré toutes les souffrances
> Je pense avec joie chaque jour
> A tous ceux qui là-bas en France
> Attendent aussi mon retour.
>
> Partir, partir rêve qui hante,
> Tu deviendras realité,
> Et c'est pour cela que je chante,
> Car l'espoir ne m'a pas quitté

Si mon coeur a saigné quand même,
Si mon corps de froid a tremblé,
Avec les miens, bonheur suprême,
Nous serons bientot rassemblés.

(The most beautiful day of my life
Will be that of my return.
When I leave Westphalia
I will come back home for ever.
Oh beautiful day, ever longed for,
For me you will be filled with rejoicing.
The best day of my life
Will be that of my return.

I wait for the end of our miseries
With patience and pride,
For I know that on this earth
Freedom will return to us,
And in spite of all the suffering,
Each day I think with joy
Of all those who there in France
Are awaiting my return too.

Depart, dream which haunts me,
You will become reality
And this is why I sing,
For hope has not left me,
Even if my heart has bled,
Though my body has shivered with cold,
With my dear ones, supreme joy,
We will soon be together again.)

The agonies of the deportation, the change in the atmosphere of the village, slowly altered Emile's character; he wanted to change his surroundings, finding no interest in his business, and not responding to the pleas of his friends in the Béziers orchestra who wanted to resume the production of *L'Arlésienne*.

Each spring day brought one or more Capestang men back to the village; 184 deportees returned to take up their places in their homes. It was a miracle that they had all survived the hardships, and above all, the bombing! Alone, Monsieur Lejbowicz was not among them; victim of his Jewish roots, his life, which had started so fruitfully, had ended in the sinister Auschwitz camp. What a dreadful waste! He bore no hatred towards anyone, he was a gentle man, discreet and extremely cultured. Musician, writer, fluent in several languages, he would certainly have enriched our heritage. He had started to write a tragedy with musical interludes, which he had just submitted to us as they were being worked on. The rhythms, clashing with percussion, disconcerted me a little, but listening to modern music today, I realise that he was a forerunner of his time.

When all those that the war had sent far away had been returned to the village, a *Fête de Retour* was organised. Prisoners and deportees with their families, united in the spirit of brotherhood, took part in a magnificent banquet and a very lively ball. On 8th May peace had returned: Germany had capitulated! That day, under a radiant sun, a burgeon of flags bearing the cross of Lorraine adorned the balconies; we would not have believed that so many partisans existed. Cockades and tricolor bows broke out on bodices and jacket lapels.

Up until then, it was dangerous to nail one's colours to the mast: now, we were liberated, we could plan ahead, and make the most of the gift of life, as for many long months –
Was it living, to have to doubt the return of those with whom we had been born and raised?
Was it living, to tremble with continuous fear for the safety of oneself and one's family?
Was it living, to be gripped with anguish at the fate which would be ours if the enemy triumphed?
Was it living, not to be able to give a piece of bread to a hungry child?
One had to have lived through this period of privation and agony to understand the explosion of joy at the announcement that all that was over. A new era was going to begin ... for those who were lucky enough to be there...

What splendid lives lost! In the foul gulf of the Nazi camps, what aborted hopes, what human riches were wiped out: and my heart contracts with pain at the thought that in the smoke of the gas ovens, the trusting childhood of three of my little pupils was borne away.

Even after so many years, one cannot forget, nor stifle the revulsion.

'Come onto the square; the girls' heads are going to be shaved.' I will not describe to you what went on. I never responded to this invitation which made me feel sick. I thought of these poor creatures who had had the weakness to succumb to the advances of a German soldier, who had to carry for long months the shameful brand of their disgrace, and keep in their hearts all their lives long, the bitter memory of the humiliation they suffered from the mocking, loathing expressions on the faces of their compatriots. There were better things to do!

It is cowardly to go to the attack of those who have no defence to satisfy the base desires for revenge.

As in all wars, there were outbursts which were often bloody, and, in the name of purging, settlings of personal scores were permitted, even to the extent of the bankruptcy of political adversaries.

* * *

In spite of the war ending, we were not much better off for supplies; the ration cards were maintained until 1948, and the daily quota of 250 grams of bread was reduced to 200 grams. The only thing our friends in Saint Pourçain lacked was ... olive oil. Thinking that we were well provided for in the Midi, they called on us for it. I had never spoken to them about the sad situation of our food shortage, but their request allowed me to put them in the picture concerning our deprivation. They were overcome, and as they had a butchery/charcuterie business in a privileged region, they sent us parcels regularly which improved our day-to-day fare.

In the long holidays they invited us to go there and make the most of their comfortable situation, and we were almost scandalised by the gastronomic luxury of the Bourbonnais. On our arrival, the sight of an abundantly laid table brought tears to our eyes. In the country, restaurants served copious 'snacks' with ham, cream tarts, etc., ... This seemed indecent to us.

159

XIX

After Emile came back, we left the modest house where so many days, both happy and sad, had been spent, to settle in a bourgeois house, Casamia, made available by the ex-mayor. There we found ourselves in relative comfort, with running water and a little courtyard enclosing the conveniences, but the neighbourhood was not as friendly as the Plan de Castres.

Nevertheless, it was there that I learnt the wonderful news that we were expecting a happy event! We had always wanted a second child. The birth was due to take place in September, and I felt at one with the vines, whose branches bent under the weight of the heavy bunches of grapes. The sun shone with nature's generosity: my baby was going to arrive: but, it was too much joy! Remi, playing bareheaded in the great heat on a stack of straw near the house had a meningeal reaction. Emile and I watched over him together for long nights in total darkness, covering his burning head with rubber bags, filled with ice. We spent very anxious hours at his bedside ... and I reproached myself for the joy I felt about the pregnancy. At last, Remi recovered, and on a hot September afternoon, our second child came into the world, this time with very little delay. A little girl! A dark Mireille, with very bright black eyes, all plump! I was overjoyed; I did not want to go to sleep and miss savouring my happiness.

To thank me for having achieved our dream, my husband gave me ... a car! That is to say, that the circumstances dictated that the purchase took place during my labour. Oh! it wasn't a luxury car – a modest, second-hand vehicle, a Peugeot 201. Nevertheless, the first time we went out in it, we felt we were the kings of the road!

A little while afterwards, my mother slipped in the corridor and broke her hip. This accident worsened her difficulty with walking and confined her to a wheelchair.

After renting for two years, we did not want to inconvenience the owner of the building who wanted to live in it during his retirement, and we decided to settle permanently in our own home. Finally, in September 1948, we moved into our own little house which we had extended into the surrounding garden. We were always happy with our choice; the house is simple but functional and we have modified it over the years to make it more comfortable. From the beginning we were able to benefit from a shower, thanks to a motor which pumped the water from the wells, a facility which many Capestanais envied ... but the neighbourhood streets had never known any refuse collection, and Emile found an opportunity to sing about this negligence in a refrain composed for the Fête d'Abreuvoir:

> Près du stade magnifique
> Habite le chef de musique
> Du quartier de l'Abreuvoir
> C'est un coin a ne pas voir.
>
> Mais quand les rues seront faites
> Il prendra un air de fête
> Et il sera dans le ton
> Grace à l'administration.
>
> (Near the splendid stadium
> Lives the conductor of the orchestra
> In the Abreuvoir neighbourhood
> Which is not fit to be seen.
>
> But when the streets are made up
> It will look marvellous
> And the tone will be raised,
> Thanks to the administration.)

But the administration were slow to complete these works; the roadway remained difficult for a long time and our shoes were often covered in mud. Our move there coincided with the time when Remi started as a secondary school pupil in Béziers; first as a boarder, and then he came home each evening. We were a big family then, as my mother-in-law had come to live permanently with us. She left us during the severe winter of 1956, in February, victim of a cerebral haemorrhage.

I had to submit to the custom which dictated that the family should be attended during the funeral watch by friends and neighbours. The intention was kindly meant, but the gathering lacked reverence. I had to pass round a large number of drinks: milk, coffee and little cakes. The later it got, the conversation, which at first was murmured in low tones and consisted of reminiscences about the life of the deceased, changed in tone and in subject, and spread to local gossip. Thankfully, at the time of my own mother's death, I didn't have to go along with this inappropriate tradition.

In spite of her handicap and her suffering, my mother lived on for another 15 years. The verandah made it possible for her to endure her immobility a little more easily, and there she would cherish her dreams, with the help of Remi, who each week at her request, brought her a tenth share in a National Lottery ticket. In advance, she had distributed her winnings so generously that she exceeded the expected total! Above all, she enjoyed the visits from people of her own age, with whom she would criticise the 'young people of today'.

During the holidays we used to take her to Saint-Thibéry, where she used to enjoy seeing her old house again, together with her sister. Different from each other though they were, they were joined together 'like a fingernail to the skin'.

My aunt was tall and sturdy, my mother was frail and sickly, and paradoxically, it was she who lived longer, justifying the Occitan saying: 'Val maï pipio qué cacaracà!' (A little bird is hardier than a splendid cockerel). But the ten years of her life without her sister lacked interest for her. Before my mother's accident, both of them took up their well loved habits in their village: the ritual knitting sessions in front of the door with their neighbours, the church services and the visits to the cemetery, where, as each year passed, their acquaintances were more numerous than in the streets of the town.

They each had the same destiny at the ends of their lives, ending their existence at ease in the homes of their daughters. When they were apart, they wrote each other long letters, in which spelling was hardly attended to, but in which they poured out their feelings with great tenderness, and freed themselves of the little irritations that they kept quiet about to us. Nowadays, Margot and I keep in touch with each other by telephone, and even though the customs have changed, I think that we carry on in much the same way.

In 1954, the climate of the nation was darkened by the Algerian uprising. Anguish once more tortured many Capestang families, who trembled for the lives of their sons who were called up.

During the conflict, Remi was a pupil at the teacher training college in Mende, and it was there that he met the person whom he married in 1958.

A Time of Joys Great and Small and also of Great Sadness

3rd Movement – Poco andante

XX

In 1960 we went to Marvejols, the first posting of our young marrieds; it was on the occasion of the birth of Nelly, who came into the world on Easter Monday, when light flakes of snow floated under the sky of the Lozère.

She was an adorable baby, with big blue eyes and a pink complexion, and I never tired of admiring her.

At 48 I was quite young to be able to revel in this beautiful gift and I made the most of it; in the holidays, her parents often entrusted me with her, and I was more than a little proud of the compliments she brought my way, for she was a truly pretty little girl.

I asked her to write to me, without getting anyone's help; she did not demur, and here is her first missive, without any alterations:

> Chaire mamie,
>
> Je te souhaite que tout le monde né pas malade; je souète que je ne pas dernière au classement cinon je norés pas mon vélo que papa vamacheté si je sui première ou 3.

> (Dear Granny,
>
> I hope that everyone is not ill; I hope I will not be bottom of the class, if so I will not have my bicycle which Daddy is going to buy me if I am in the first three.)

As our visits to Saint-Thibéry became less frequent, my mother encouraged us to sell her house. All my childhood memories were there, and each room resonated with my past;

the happy days of my adolescence surrounded by the loving concern of my parents, the joyful atmosphere of the *jours de fête*, but also my distress over the love which had been thwarted at one time; there I had nearly died at 20 years old, and there, one sad October day, Death had arrived and borne away prematurely a much loved father...

The packing up was a chance for a monumental clear out: a little pile of ashes in the garden was all that was left of exercise books, newspapers, books, outdated clothes and heavy curtains. Emile felt encumbered with it all and a big distribution to our close relatives followed. An imposing cupboard with metal fittings, a smaller one with richly decorated doors, a solid walnut bedstead 'for one and a half people' (sic), were excellent bargains for the antique dealers.

We had no regrets at getting rid of the bedside tables which we considered to be of no use from now on, for they contained the chamber pot, a utensil which had been of great value in satisfying urgent nocturnal needs, but had lost its purpose thanks to modern conveniences.

Remi ended the clearing out at the municipal dump; to 'ease my sorrows', he finished off the opaline lamp shade with a blow from a hammer, and I felt my heart lurch as I heard the final cracked strike of an old clock, forever condemned to silence.

It is true that we would have had great difficulty in finding room for all these things, but I reproach myself for getting rid of the evidence of my youth, and for having allowed documents so well preserved and carefully filed by my father to be destroyed ... New occupants moved in to our home, completely changing the decor, and in 1963 we bought an apartment at Valras, a seaside resort near Capestang. This practical and well-designed ground-floor flat suited us perfectly and we spent some wonderful holidays there. My mother was able to enjoy a beneficial change of scene, and installed on the terrace, she made the most of the friendly neighbourhood. When we first went there, there was still a block of waste land opposite our building which we used to cross to gain easy access to the beach.

In the mornings I would go there and pick wild flowers which made pretty country bouquets; and the only sound in the evenings was the song of the crickets hidden in the tall grasses.

The building of an apartment block put an end to this rural idyll, but our cul-de-sac is still welcoming and remains a favourite place for the children to play games. Nelly was the first to benefit enormously from these pleasant surroundings and the delights of the beach.

After we had been there several years, in order to strengthen bonds with our neighbours, we took the initiative of instigating a communal meal. Emile suggested to the mayor, Monsieur Turco, that we should name our *impasse* after Yves Nat, who was a well-known pianist from Béziers; we conducted this ceremony with great pomp: the oldest inhabitant in the neighbourhood, wrapped in a shawl, cut the tricolor ribbon which was across the road to the strains of a vibrant Marseillaise, played by my husband on his violin; then we processed to take our places round the tables which were laid ready in the open air; the brightly coloured tablecloths added an extra touch of jollity. A string of multicoloured light bulbs, lent by our neighbour who was a cabinet-maker, provided light for the 70 guests. A glass of sangria set everyone going, and pizzas, *omelettes flambées*, grilled sausages, cheeses, fruit and gâteaux followed one another, interspersed with songs and anecdotes; it was all washed down with our own good wine. Towards midnight, all the tables were pushed back and the floor was ready for a dance which was improvised till dawn. It was a really good evening after which friendships between all in the neighbourhood became closer.

I used to make the most of the pleasures of the beach: bathing, and chatting while comfortably installed in the shade of parasols, on the sand.

Emile, for his part, having completely given up going into the sea since he had pulled a drowned person out from it, took advantage of my absence to smoke forbidden cigarettes, with a notebook and pencil in his hand; perhaps it was in the smoke of this tobacco, his great weakness, that he discovered his most pungent witticisms and his richest rhymes...

The day would end pleasantly, for the esplanade by the sea front was a meeting place and somewhere to walk, where one could prolong the evenings while enjoying the fresh sea breeze after the intense heat of the day. Our friendship with Monsieur Turco resulted in us benefiting from a wide range of shows at the seaside theatre. We used to be his guests at the artistic events of the Festival de la Côte Languedocienne, and we had the much appreciated honour of attending wonderful concerts at Sérignan and Béziers.

Mireille was thrilled to spend two months' holiday at Valras, where she was free to make new friendships which were added interest for her during her stay. Paradoxically, it was there that she got to know a group of young people from Capestang, and this was the start of her romance with Pierrot. Their wedding took place in December 1967, amid a crowd of relations and friends, all happy to celebrate a young couple who were much liked in the village.

Their first joy was the birth of Florence, which was preceded by the arrival of Nathalie in Remi's home. They came into the world during the anti-establishment period of 1968.

XXI

I took up my retirement the following year. My mother was anxious to have me with her more. I felt a pang of sadness at leaving my life of service to children; they kept my dynamism going and communicated their *joie de vivre*; we ended the school year with a large public *fête* at the town stadium, and I felt at one with them in their excitement and delight.

It was during the last act of the show, where some mischievous little rabbits chased one another through the cabbages, and after the graceful arabesques of the skaters, that the dignitaries and my colleagues kindly made a presentation to me. I was deeply appreciative of their tributes, but I was especially moved when all the children of my school, their arms filled with flowers, crowded on to the stage to sing 'Adieu, Monsieur le professeur'.

I wanted to leave a last message to all my pupils who were there (some of whom were in their 40s):

> You are living at an exciting time, but its whirlwind scarcely leaves space for simple pleasures. Know then, my children, to appreciate the things which are closest to you; don't put on a veneer of scepticism which does you harm; trust in the goodness of those who are all around you.
>
> The great pacifist Gandhi, who loved his fellow men, said: 'You must never lose faith in humanity; it is like an ocean; a few drops of dirty water cannot contaminate it entirely.'
>
> Rediscover the enthusiasm of your childhood. I give you back all that you have given me, and even if only one amongst you takes it to brighten his life, the 34 years

171

I have lived in this village, to which I have given much, but from which I have also gained a great deal, will not have been in vain.

A few days later, I found by my garden gate an envelope held down by four pebbles, which contained a drawing and these few words: 'Mme Bélet, je regrette mon frere et moi de vous avoir quitter' (sic). (Mme Bélet, my brother and I are sorry to have left you.)

This little missive was followed by other acts of thoughtfulness, which made all my efforts worthwhile.

* * *

After Remi had been head of the college at La Canourgue, he went to live at Carcassonne where other duties awaited him. Being nearer to Capestang made visits easier, and Florence and Nathalie, who were almost the same age, were delighted to meet each other regularly. My retired status gave me the opportunity to put aside lots of time for them. Though they had different temperaments, they played extremely well together. They adored playing at tea parties with real crockery and real food; they even tried out, with my supervision, some slightly strange cooking, which thrilled them.

I had made some marionettes which performed traditional fairy tales and stories which I made up. Sometimes the little girls came behind the curtain, but discovering the game did not taint their innocence and they were a devoted audience.

What joy they had when I allowed them to go up into the attic! There was always something amazing to discover. A little cupboard, where I had stored outdated dresses and hats, was regularly pillaged: Nelly was mistress of ceremonies, and they followed her out into the garden amid loud laughter, walking unsteadily on high heels, hampered in long skirts, and the proudest was the one wearing a certain white hat, called, I can't think why, 'le chapeau de printemps', which was a particular favourite.

What wonderful times I have spent with these three children. With them, the traditional festivals took on a special glow. Christmas is a delight: the secret preparations in advance are already a happy prelude to the joys which follow. With

172

much excitement we put up the garlands which run along the walls and unfurl round the branches of the Christmas tree ... the house must be gay and bright. Putting out the presents, we have advance pleasure at the children's surprise; our expectation is as feverish as theirs, we long to be quietly present at their bursts of joy.

At Easter, we used to follow the tradition of hunting for eggs in the garden; with little baskets tucked under their arms, off the children went on the search; wisely, *les cloches* had not let anything fall round the rose bushes, so that the prickles would not hurt small fingers ... but the clump of tulips hid a bounty, and many flowers lost their petals in the invasion of avid hands; a few presents were out of reach and stayed hung up on the branches of the cedar tree; there they were protected from the onslaught of the dogs who, all excited by the atmosphere, ran round the children and ate some of the sweets. Over the years the Easter manna was augmented with toys and books and the result of the pickings was evaluated with greater interest; some exchanges were made according to taste, but however rich the harvest, the hunting and the discovery were the most fun of all.

It was after one of these celebrations, in April 1971, that my mother left us, very quietly, at the age of 92. For some time she had hardly taken much part in family life; these gatherings which she used to enjoy so much, made her unwell: 'When they are there,' she used to say, 'you are only busy with *them*.' She had closed her eyes during the showing of the film which Remi had made of the very happy celebration of her 90th birthday, showing the lack of interest which she felt in it all. This abnegation did not correspond to her warm nature nor her great love for her family. She adored the children and always took care to have sweets in her pockets to give them. They had all been rocked to sleep by the 'Chanson de bon petit Lucas', in a voice which still sounded youthful. I think that she was weary of living ... for such a long time her body had been racked with 'aches and pains' which she bore with difficulty, despite the pain-killers. A great part of our married life was spent with our mothers. Their presence was valuable for our children, for whom there was always someone at home to play with, and they were a great help to me.

173

My mother died on 28th April, on her wedding anniversary, the day she had been so happy to fulfil her dreams. The lines had disappeared from her sorrowful face, she looked serene and had recovered a certain youthfulness.

I did not get over her death quickly; she had been my companion through life and her delicate health had attached me the more strongly to her through the constant care she needed from me.

I would have continued willingly to look after her for much longer, but I had to accept the outcome, and to realise that it was, all the same, high time, in my 60th year, to lead an independent life as a couple, free to make plans and to carry them out. We allowed ourselves to do this, and the first thing I did was to satisfy my longing to travel with a visit to Austria. Emile was not curious about new horizons; very simple in his tastes, his home surroundings were enough for him and it was there that he found his happiness, but he agreed to come with me, and year after year I dragged him along – to Italy (to Venice), Spain, Portugal, Holland, Denmark, Corsica and Brittany. With his poetic nature always on the alert, during these changes of scenery, he found an appeal in preparing ways to liven up the long journeys. We used to engage the services of a local tour travel company, and our group consisted mostly of people from Capestang. Without much protest, I became my husband's performing partner, and our travelling relationship was made to sparkle with songs, poems and sketches made up on the spot, and recalling our doings in the manner of cabaret singers. The bus was driven by our friend André Bru, a very knowledgeable guide, concerned for our comfort and the cultural richness of our trips. By word of mouth, his reputation spread, and we acquired a following of intellectuals from Montpellier who were delighted to join us. We used to return exhausted from the voyage of discovery, but happy, enriched with a certain philosophy and ready to set off again, for, as Emile concluded:

> On en parle ... très a l'avance,
> On en jouit lors du séjour,
> Au retour souvent l'on y pense
> Puissions nous voyager toujours!

(We talk about it ... long before,
We enjoy it at the time
We think of it often after our return
If only we could travel for ever!)

We appreciated travelling as part of a group: some people regretted having to conform to a set itinerary. But this was compensated for by the fact that we set off free from any worries about where we were going to stay: the stop was organised, the sightseeing prepared in advance, and this allowed us to enjoy as much as possible in the minimum time, which would have been impossible as individuals. We would have the opportunity to stop off at a comfortable place when needed. Leading this communal life for a whole fortnight demanded a certain compromise; it shed light on the attitudes of our travelling companions and kept some surprises in reserve! ... Life in community is not always easy!

We must be glad that the development of these tours has enabled many people, often towards the ends of their lives, to enlarge their horizons and, thanks to these escapes, forget their troubles.

* * *

In our home, too many chairs were vacant now around our table; our mothers had left us, and our children had gone to bring up their own families. Mireille was not very far away; she had chosen our neighbourhood in which to build her house; even though it was comfortable and well designed inside, she found life as a housewife monotonous, and longed for an occupation in which she could achieve her potential. With enthusiasm, she accepted the job as secretary to the Capestang college, then at Saint-Pons and later on at Narbonne. Her absences left us in charge of looking after Florence.

Emile would not let anyone else be responsible for taking her to school, while I prepared her favourite meals. I have kept the little books of stories that I used to tell her.

I little thought then that these simple writings, and the recordings of the first piece she played on the piano, and the recitations by both Nathalie and Florence would be so precious to me one day ... They both spoke beautifully and I still

175

enjoy listening to it. Florence's long stay with us gave her certain privileges, and she claimed ownership of the games by writing her name clearly on the boxes, quickly challenged by Nathalie who added her own name! This unvoiced silent rivalry greatly amused me. Later I followed Florence through her secondary schooling and once again enjoyed going through the curriculum, as I had done seriously with Remi, and to a lesser extent with Mireille – I used to become excessively alarmed at her fragile appearance – but as a grandmother I had more patience and receptiveness. Florence was a source of activity and joy in our retirement.

Emile kept busy as usual – rather half-heartedly – with his little vineyard. We no longer had to worry about the *cave* since the building of the cooperative in 1936, but the sale of the wine was uncertain. The members of the cooperative had not adopted the communal sale which my husband supported; he thought that this was important for a better profit. So the dealers made offers which were signalled by the *pompiers'* siren and broadcast over the town's loudspeaker. This caused much dithering. We used to decide to take what was offered, even if the prices showed an upward trend a few days later.

This provoked talk amongst some households. It was important for many families to get the maximum from their only source of income.

We had never had a great deal of luck in business affairs and our sales had not been among the best ... but this was not a catastrophe, as we were not wholly reliant on the money; our simple tastes were within our means, and my teacher's salary ensured our day-to-day fare.

Today, good sense has prevailed, and it is an administrative council, uniting several wine-growing communes which makes the decisions over accepting the prices offered and fixes the amount of the sale. These elected representatives have the trust of the members of the cooperative, who are relieved at last of this major worry.

Emile was not a great spender, but, paradoxically, he was the first to purchase innovations which made home life easier. This resulted in numerous callers; some sceptical people came to watch the working of the pressure cooker – supposed to be injurious to health – the washing machine (didn't the buttons

176

come off?), and the dishwasher (weren't the glasses broken?). Bypassing the 'icebox', we had graduated from 'putting it in the cool' in the well, to the Frigidaire; people ironically called us the 'nouveaux riches'. Nowadays all these items of equipment have become commonplace and are in almost every home.

XXII

At the end of my teaching career in June 1969, when all my colleagues in education, from the infant school through to the primary school (not one was left out) came to offer me their best wishes with a delightful memento, I said to them: 'I do not consider retirement as an ending, but as a second beginning; retirement means to be active in freedom.'

I have been faithful to this vow, and for 25 years I have not ceased to put myself to the service of others. First of all I tended towards helping the elderly, and I took part in starting a group for them – we hadn't started talking of the 'Club du 3me âge' in those days.

When the Foyer Rural began, I suggested that elderly people should be taken in there, within the walls of the old castle. This was not easy, and this lodging gave rise to hearty criticism from several sides. Nevertheless, a meeting place was needed to overcome the isolation of old people, to make contact with them and to inform them of their entitlements and how they could obtain them. Our aims were modest, at the beginning, and later we organised a few activities, some little intimate parties, day trips, and a glimpse of the outer world with some amateur film shows etc., ... Over the years the '3me âge' has become an institution, and we have contacts with departmental and national groups; this meant a lot of correspondence, where a little of our reputation crept in, and travel agents, for whom we were heaven-sent, sent us alluring invitations.

Little by little our association made a name for itself, and we were able to join with the young people to participate in the life of the village: preparing *fêtes* with decorated floats, putting on local dancing displays etc.

The spirit was freely given and I rejoiced in the warmth of the weekly meetings, finding a friendship and esteem there which more than rewarded the hours of work which I put in. There were some very elderly people amongst us and the trust which they placed in me made me give all I could, and willingly.

Sometimes I would be particularly touched by spontaneous gestures such as this one: our club had been invited to a free performance by Marcel Reval at the town theatre in Béziers; in the interval one old granny of 85 brought me a chocolate ice-cream, and said, in reply to my protestations: 'Lou meritatz; es lo primièr cop que veni al teatre.' (You deserve it; this is the first time I've ever been to the theatre.)

It is impossible to predict how future generations will develop; the grandson of our old lady who was so far removed from artistic life, became a brilliant dancer at the Opéra de Paris, and will doubtless perform on the most splendid platforms in the world: his name is José Valls.

Emile and I shared a love of performing and we were able to fulfil this in these friendly gatherings. Our repertoire had the advantage of being original, and we had as much pleasure in preparing as performing it. Over a period of ten years, along with other really talented people in the group, we provided entertainment at all our *fêtes* and journeys.

As well as this, we gathered singers from different generations to form a mixed four-part choir; we used to meet once a week, finding a great deal of pleasure in this form of expression, where one joined in an ensemble, and where one's own voice seemed enhanced. We only benefited from a few years of the varied programme directed by Emile; we had to abandon these pleasant study evenings, powerless against the competition of the television which kept our singers in their own homes, to enjoy an easier pleasure. It was but a fleeting happiness which we still remember with nostalgia.

Later on, the 3me âge clubs abounded in all the communes, and as they were avid for entertainment, we were asked as a pair to go to enliven parties, banquets and soirées. Free of all constraint, we responded enthusiastically with our voluntary support; our programme, consisting mainly of poems, songs, double acts and sketches that we had made up ourselves, lasted two hours. Our reputation spread quickly, and we were unable to meet all the demands. We discovered attractive places and made some interesting friends. Like simple, modern day troubadours, we used to set off happily, with our heads full of songs, ready for the warm reception. I overtired my throat which was always a bit delicate and sometimes let me down in spite of all I could do, but I could not give up these sessions which were always so satisfying to us. We used to return enriched with the happiness that we had given. The fact that we were actually a couple who were married to each other contributed no little to our success, and people envied our perfect harmony and *joie de vivre.*

I had kept up my contacts with the school: having been appointed departmental representative of the national infant education where I had worked for 33 years, I was put in charge of seeing to the safety and well-being of the children, and of maintaining the links between the school, the family and the social environment. This function pleased me all the more as it was facilitated by the cooperation of a dependable staff who contributed to the excellent running of the establishment.

I was happy to find myself back in the setting which had been so familiar to me, noting with pleasure that nothing of my time there had been renounced, and rejoicing at the positive changes. I recalled the memory of departed colleagues, and those who had gone far away, with whom I used to make professional and friendly links. In the playground still floats the frail spectre of Rosine, our first cleaner, and all those other equally dedicated ladies who followed her. How often have I stepped through this heavy door to go and meet the children! I worked in all the classrooms, and each one reminded me of the little happenings of a particular stage of my career. The echoes of our songs filled the playground. It was round this tree that we danced in happy circles. It was in this sunny corner that we huddled close together in a group, to watch (with what feelings!) the arrival of the Inspector General accompanied by the departmental chief. It was not until after her visit, followed by congratulations, that we realised what an honour had been accorded to us.

The children still behave the same, a little more restless

perhaps, or have I become more sensitive to noise? Dark faces, with beautiful black eyes, now mingle with those of our own young children in whom I recognise characteristics that remind me of their parents...

All these pleasant occupations have made up for leaving my profession, and I have never experienced boredom. It was a happy retirement in which we achieved what we wanted. Nevertheless, it was sadly scarred by upheavals which took place in the homes of our two children.

Don't let anyone tell me that divorce is a trivial thing. I felt bruised all over and, deep down, for ever bear the marks of this double heartbreak which has disrupted the lives of people who had been close to me for a long time and to whom I was genuinely attached, and above all, the lives of my grand-daughters, so dear to my heart.

XXIII

At the same time as this was going on, Emile's health gave rise to serious problems. Despite alarming investigations and repeated advice, he had not given up tobacco, and often satisfied his longing in secret. This resulted in a lung disfunction and severe inflammation of the arteries; his epiglottis was reduced to a third of its size, and while we awaited the results of tests we lived in the fear of cancer. It was tuberculosis.

It seems astonishing to rejoice at such news, but nevertheless this was the case, for this illness, which is quite rare these days, is curable. I looked after him at home, emptying the house as Mireille and Florence had found somewhere else to go, and I was isolated for long months with my patient, and we conquered the disease.

All these shocks had an effect on my much needed good health: I discovered a lump in my left breast, and an immediate mammography revealed a tumour and resulted in my having to have radiation treatment. I had to face this in difficult circumstances; that January it was snowing, the ground was icy, and Emile's condition meant that he could not accompany me. I kept up my courage, and in the waiting room my optimism even reassured the other people there. At the end of March I went in to the St Eloi clinic in Montpellier, where I shared a room with a delightful person. The first examination was different for each of us:

'You,' said the doctor to my companion, 'will be quick, just a few cysts to remove!'

'As for you,' he said to me, 'we're going to take everything away. Did you know?'

No, I had not known, but if it had to be ...

The next day I was sent to the surgical block. I left anxious faces behind me. Apart from Emile, and Florence and Nathalie whom we had sent away, all my loved ones were there.

I am calm; there are long minutes of waiting and then I am pushed towards the 'dissecting' chamber; this word comes to me from memories of my experiments at the *école normale* when I used to carve up little animals under anaesthetic. I find myself under an enormous light; the moment I have dreaded for three whole months is about to happen; my heart beats faster; lots of people dressed in white bustle around me, impatient to mutilate me, it seems. An injection; the needle goes in properly after a clumsy first attempt; a black rubber mask is put over my face and brings me oblivion; I sink into nothingness; this then, is death, it is not so terrible after all . . .

With a greenish complexion, my lips sunken on an empty jaw, I find myself back in my hospital bed; there is a confused sound of voices . . . I open one eye; I come to from time to time; a tube hurts my throat. I attempt a moan; I call for help: 'I'm suffocating, I'm thirsty.' I realise that those around me, despite wanting to, are powerless to give me relief. I have to suffer alone this terrible sensation of suffocation, this dreadful, excruciating pain in my arm, and this thirst which makes me think of those who die of it in the desert. They would have mercy on me! I try again: 'I'm suffocating! I'm thirsty!' A nurse says to me, magnanimously: 'You will have a little water at midnight!' and it is two o'clock in the afternoon . . . This dreadful day is followed by a night that is even more painful and seems never-ending. I have to endure it on my own; the crampedness of the room doesn't allow for the presence of one of my family. It is my room mate's husband who moistens my lips, changes my position, raises my pillow. At last the pale dawn comes; it looks as if it will be a glorious day; in spite of everything it is good to be alive; it is my birthday, and I am 73.

I recovered my form, and two days later I took a walk in the park, to the surprise of friends and relatives who came to see me. Afterwards I was transferred to Val d'Aurelle; my hospital neighbours saw me leave with regret, for I got up little concerts for them which kept up their spirits. Comfortably settled in the new establishment in a spacious room, I made friends with the nurses who were amazed at my dynamism, and eight days after my return to Capestang, I was organising a sports day for retired people in the department.

Afterwards, however, I felt the need for a complete rest, which was necessary, too, for Emile, and we were both admitted to the Osséja pneumology centre in the Eastern Pyrénées. It was Remi who arranged for us to go to this pleasant spot, where I spent a delightful stay: the countryside is glorious, the air light and fresh; I got to know interesting people there, and we went for walks together around the nearby lake, or in the forest where the pine trees rose beside the road bordered with lupins of all colours, or by car to Font Romeu and Mont Louis. I had regular medical checks, and a suspect patch was discovered on my right lung. My Béziers doctor, informed of this, made me undergo a bronchoscopy which revealed a fibrous lesion caused by the radiation treatment.

Since then, its development has been monitored, along with the follow up of my operation. These visits are reassuring and a tonic, and renew my confidence for a year.

* * *

If, up till now, I have had no sequel to this incident, it was not the same for Emile, whose health deteriorated more and more. Walking was painful for him, he went out very little, and his sparkle had disappeared. The only interest he showed was in the Foyer Rural, up the steps of which he struggled with difficulty; there he found the echo of his poetry creations, and an esteem which reassured him. After his long absence from social life, he had been very touched by the demonstrations of sympathy towards him as he made contact with people again. As much as his strength would allow, he went in to the schools to show his concern for the state education, and he was there, the day before his stroke, to applaud the introduction of the computer system.

He was struck with partial paralysis, and his condition necessitated his transfer to hospital, where he lived out his last fortnight – a time which I would rather have effaced from our lives as it was so distressing for us both. He could no longer speak, and his eyes expressed only resentment and outrage.

All the family came, as far as they were able, to gather

184

round our beloved patient, but he died completely alone, in the middle of the night, without the touch of a loving hand or words of comfort. This thought is still unbearable for me ... The day before, the doctor on duty had been reassuring and was talking about rehabilitation in a specialist establishment ... I have borne most ordeals well, but this one was the most painful of all. How would I carry on living without the one with whom I had shared everything with so much trust and so much love ... and above all how would I come to terms with knowing that he would have none of the happiness of watching his grandchildren grow up, whom he loved so dearly? They used to call him 'papiche' with affection, for he was like no other grandfather. He was refreshing to live with; with his artistic nature, blossoming within his music and song; he was happy without being ambitious; he dismissed all anxiety and whenever gossip was aimed at him, an ironic poem, quickly dashed off, used to be his only revenge.

His civic funeral was very moving: the town orchestra, made up of the pupils he had built up with such devotion, played with fervour the funeral march which he had conducted so many times and now would never hear again. I felt overwhelmed at the sound of it, but did not allow my grief to take over; I would have time to weep in my solitude. It was important to thank fittingly this thoughtful throng who had come, some from a very long distance, to express all the esteem and gratitude which they owed him. I listened with contained emotion to the eulogy spoken by the president of the national education delegates, whom he had helped so much with his support: 'Without thought for his own interests, seeking neither praise nor thanks, he wished only to be regarded as one loyal to and trusting in our ideal, which he intended to affirm, continue and defend with his ardent faith of the convinced militant.'

The public whom he had delighted and entertained in the surrounding villages were there, and I know that he would not have been shocked – he would even have been happy – if one of his songs had been hummed in the cortège.

XXIV

I began my solitary life in this house which he had planned with so much love, and which, though simple, fulfilled all his wishes. Biter, the spaniel that we had had for 15 years, is my companion, and we grow old together. He is demanding, follows my every step and protests loudly when I leave him; but on my return I am sure to be welcomed with wild enthusiasm; his company is a reassurance and we live in a permanent collusion.

I do not allow myself to be beaten; I took up my activities with the senior citizens of the village once more, and with a few neighbouring clubs who asked for my support.

But like everything, at the end of so many years, our associations changed; the number of very old people diminished, replaced by pre-retired people who wanted other kinds of activities: pre-1940s dances, longer trips etc., ... The atmosphere is still just as friendly, but the need for concern for their welfare is less.

So I can, without being accused of desertion, leave it to someone younger who will know how to respond to these new aims. For 15 years I gave up many things and a part of my personal life to the running of the club. It is time that I am able to respond, without demur, to the invitations of my own family.

After the shocks which were aroused and gone through, the families had been reconstituted elsewhere in different settings, and the two new homes had each been enriched by the arrival of sons who fulfilled our expectations: Mathieu and Numa.

Nelly's marriage had elevated us to the ranks of great-grandparents with the arrival of three adorable little girls, and all this little world jostles about in my heart, which is already full with the dear ones who have gone before.

So I have three happy homes to welcome me; my solitude is not painful to me, for I know that I can break it whenever I wish.

In spite of all the pleasure that I get from these visits away to the family, I really like to stay at home; I like the comfort and amenities of my house where I have many things to do, and I am happy when no outside obligation comes to disturb my day. I tend my indoor plants which bloom happily in the warmth of my verandah. My garden, although quite scaled down, needs quite a bit of work, and each plant is an expression of life, which depends on the attention one gives to it, and its growth is a source of joy. Indoors, there are so many things to do which entice me! I never stop having new interests and I never exhaust them.

At the age of 73, confined to the house for a long time during Emile's illness, I started to learn the piano. It was pretentious of me, but it was something I had wanted to do for a long time! I took the advice of J. Delteil who said: 'Follow your dream.' Jo, Emile's pupil, who continued the direction of the town orchestra, had kindly given me the simplified scores of classical pieces by Gounod, Strauss, Boccherini, Rameau, Chopin etc., ... I set myself valiantly to the task, and Emile's less than eulogistic comments did not deter me. I would never dare to appear in front of an audience, but my playing is good enough to give me pleasure, and each time she comes, one of my friends is happy to listen to her favourite piece: 'La Valse' by Brahms. In this study, which demanded my concentrated attention in a number of ways, I found a means of distracting myself from the cares which beset me, and of dissipating the grip of too oppressive a silence.

It is certainly exciting to hear a lovely piece of music being played, but nothing is equal to the pleasure of making it come to life under one's own fingers.

I also write verses, which are more messages than soaring flights of poetry. They are reflections of my personality and express my affections, enthusiasms, and my outrage.

Another task is to pass on Emile's unpublished works. I am

187

transcribing all these verses which had been 'thrown to the devil' on scraps of crumpled paper, some of which are indecipherable.

The musical society having asked for his songs, I must undertake this work, which is tedious as certain tempos are half obliterated. He used to compose anywhere, with whatever materials were at hand, and would often write in the margin of the daily newspaper! I would very much like to finish this tribute that I owe him, properly. Will I have the time?

As well as the shining memories that I have of our life together, he has left me riches in the outpourings of his thoughts and of his musical culture. Thanks to these, he is always there, and it is a pleasure to sort them out, to re-read his writings, and to sight-read (after several attempts) his compositions at the piano. When they are scribbles with which I am struggling desperately, I surprise myself by saying 'Emile, it's the same as ever, this is just too much!', and then I feel privileged to be able to continue. I am not the only one who does it, for on countless occasions, at local events, people refer to all he gave to the village.

In the *lycées* in Béziers and Narbonne, some of his poems were put forward for study of the Occitan language.

He left his mark behind, and it is not a gloomy one ... but he did not have the pleasure of seeing a dream fulfilled, which had haunted us for a long time and caused us a great deal of anxiety. The school equipment in the village was deplorable, and we thought it unfair that the Capestang children should be the poor relations of the canton when it came to educational material. Together we battled in various ways without result: aborted hopes which did not shake our convictions nor discourage our efforts.

At long last, by the magic of municipal motivation which grew in strength over the years, all our schools changed their appearance almost simultaneously, and we are very proud of a *collége* which measures up to the modern technology and is provided with a splendidly equipped gymnasium, a mixed primary school which is attractive and functional, and an entirely renovated infant school on a new site. In my continued role as departmental delegate, I no longer go into my old familiar haunts, but I do not regret the fact that our small children are flourishing in surroundings that are well equipped to cater for their needs.

I am lucky to be living my retirement in the village where I spent the greater part of my life, and where I practised my profession for 33 years. My pupils are now grown up; some of them are grandparents. I think they know that I loved and respected them greatly; it is a mutual pleasure when we meet one another, and they recall tenderly their happy time in the *maternelle*. I am aware that they appreciate my taking part in the life of the village, and in recent years, they have involved me in a first theatrical production. I had great joy in sharing their feelings, and in the euphoria of success. This venture has twice put me alongside then in all the planning involved, and is a great recipe for rejuvenation.

Each year, the class celebrating its 40th anniversary, gets together for a reunion, and these are pleasant events, reuniting those whose lives have taken then far away from the village. They kindly invite their old teachers to this gathering; to thank them for this considerate thought, I dedicate this poem which I wrote especially for them; some of them showed great emotion on hearing it:

Les nombreux rendez-vous que je vous ai donnés
Sont peut-être oubliés.

La maison était vieille, avec quelques lézardes
Bien modeste la cour, où le soleil s'attarde
Mais, dès que votre troupe turbulente et rieuse
Envahissait ses murs ternes et décrépis
Aussitôt rajeunie, elle reprenait vie
Fidèle à votre rythme et d'une humeur joyeuse

Les nombreux rendez-vous que je vous ai donnés...

Oh! vous n'y veniez pas toujours très volontiers
Il fallait qu'une main bien ferme vous entraîne
Et bien que j'ai consoler votre peine
C'est toujours avec joie que tous vous me quittiez
Vers des bras plus aimants: les bras d'une maman.

Quand la folie meurtrière secoua notre monde
La cour retentissait de vos jeux, de vos rondes
Et c'est dans vos yeux clairs, tout remplis d'innocence
Que j'ai gardé la foi, contre toute espérance
Et si le front serein et le coeur affermi
J'ai traversé ce dur passage de ma vie
Aux enfants de ce temps, je dois un grand merci!

Comme toute famille, nous avons eu nos deuils
Accidents, maladies ont fermé des cercueils
Et trois de nos enfants ont brulé à Auschwitz
Pour expier le crime d'avoir un nom trop juif
Pour tous les rendez-vous dont on les a privés
Je les ai mieux aimés!

Entre la belle église, la mairie renovée
Notre école a toujours son visage discret
Mais le temps s'écoulant, le nôtre a bien changé
Le vôtre resplendit de sa belle jeunesse
Le mien n'est plus celui de la jeune maîtresse
Passant devant l'école, pensez que dans ces murs
Des gens vous ont aimés d'un amour le plus pur

A tous les rendez-vous qu'ils vous avaient donnés
Et jamais oubliés.

(The many meetings I have had with you
Are perhaps forgotten

The house was old, home to a few lizards,
With a small courtyard, where the sun lingered.
But as soon as your boisterous, laughing throng
Invaded its gloomy, crumbling walls,
It immediately felt younger, came to life,
Keeping pace with you, in joyful mood

So many meetings I have had with you...

Oh! You did not always come willingly
A very firm hand had to drag you along,

190

And even though I knew how to comfort you,
You always used to leave me joyfully
For more loving arms – the arms of a mother.

When murderous madness shook our world
The playground was full of the sound of your games and
    roundels,
And it was in your clear eyes, so full of innocence,
That I kept my faith, against all hope,
And if with serene brow and strengthened heart
I survived this difficult period of my life,
I owe great thanks to the children of those days.

Like every family, we had our griefs,
Accidents and illness have sealed some tombs
And three of our children burned in Auschwitz
To pay for the crime of a too-Jewish name.
For all the meetings which they missed
I loved them all the more!

Between the beautiful church and the renovated *mairie*,
Our school still shows its unobtrusive face
But time passes, and ours have greatly changed,
Yours resplendent in your youthfulness,
Mine no longer that of the young school mistress.
As you pass by, remember that in these walls,
There were those who loved you with the purest love

And think of the meetings that they had with you
And never forgot.)

The municipal band, too, entrusted me with introducing
their concerts; I find it a great privilege thus to serve the music
in which I have been immersed since my childhood.

It is a refuge for me always, and through it, I am reunited
with my dear departed ones who loved it so passionately.
Listening to it, everything becomes beautiful, noble, desirable.
It is a world of joy and emotion: 'it communicates to the soul a
burning desire to love.' It is the accompaniment to all life, and
its many facets fulfil all our inmost needs.

One is very fortunate when one knows how to appreciate it and to allow the waves of sound to infiltrate one's being. I feel sorry for those who are not open to its magic; I hope that it will be made more possible for children to benefit from the knowledge of music; this will build a store of joy for the future.

Nowadays, I take delight in the flourishing of instrumental ensembles and choirs which are bringing a new spirit to music-making.

I am particularly happy that we have a talented musician in the family: Jean Michel, Margot's grandson, who has chosen the same instrument as Emile to take part in top class symphony concerts. He does credit to our young generation.

I do not know what musical gifts there are in my own descendants, but, for the moment, as soon as they arrive at my house, it's a veritable tornado: one of them strums on the piano, another plucks the strings of the mandolin, they even blow down my father's tuba ... Some weekends they all get together at my home, and the adults are accompanied by seven children and three dogs: my poor Biter, who feels his age, takes refuge under my legs to avoid the energy of Tiger, Nelly's bitch, and the vigorous onslaughts of Mik, Remi's setter. The garden suffers from their tearing around and the children's frolics: the branches of the cedar tree lend themselves as a climbing frame, the bicycles criss-cross the lawn, and the ball bounces in amongst the plants!

The youngest ones prefer to be inside, and the corner of the library which is set aside for them is ransacked; the games, books and puzzles are scattered on the carpet where they play very comfortably. They are allowed to get away with lots of things at Granny's house, even searching through the bureau which contains a wealth of hidden treasures. There are cries of joy at each discovery, scrambles and laughter. While this is going on, the parents talk animatedly together, completely immersed in their own world: the subject is often school problems.

I observe all this unaccustomed activity which goes to my head a little ... but they are all happy. And so am I: I prepare these family reunions with much care, rediscovering a taste for cooking which is one of my hobbies, and I concoct tempting dishes which form a large part of the pleasures of the day.

After these moments when the house has throbbed with vibrant life, I find myself a bit distraught and the silence weighs heavily.

The hard thing about being on one's own is that one can no longer share anything; but I must in all honesty admit that there are some advantages: one is freed from family servitude; one benefits from a freedom and noticeable independence; one can lead life at one's own pace and according to one's mood.

I still keep up the summer holidays at Valras Plage, where each year I have the pleasure of returning to that friendly atmosphere.

Having been in the neighbourhood for nearly 30 years, we have watched several generations growing up. There have been several changes of ownership in the building since we first came.

Whatever their reasons for leaving, our ex-neighbours never forget their time there and regularly ask me for 'holiday' news. They have happy memories of those days, and it is with emotion that they come back to pay a short visit to the place in which they were young parents.

Firm friendships were forged within these walls, particularly amongst residents who lived in the Aveyron, Doubs, Tarn and Var. I think of them all as a little part of my family, and follow their children's progress with interest, delighting in their success.

Such a long time of communal holidays has also created strong links with the owners of the villa opposite our block of apartments. They emphasise how time has flown: Michel, the good-looking grandson, so adored by his grandmother when we moved in, has become the very responsible father of three pretty little girls who merrily liven up the cul-de-sac. His young family has taken the place of previous ones, but I know I can rely on them as I did on their parents. These precious friendships compensate in part for the empty spaces around me. The Turcos, who held such an important place in the resort, have left us; my heart is wrung when I pass their house which was so hospitable, and where we had times of such affectionate understanding; on my walks along the sea front, where we used to have such pleasant meetings, the people of my age are no longer there: have they disappeared, are they ill, or just confined to their homes?

I hope that for a long time to come, I will continue to have the company of my three friends who share my love of the sea, and the pleasure of reminiscing about our studious young days.

The passion for the sea that I felt in my childhood still remains. On my arrival I inhale with delight the iodine-filled air, evoking the taste of shellfish of which I am very fond. Then I go towards it, with its ever-changing aspect; I never tire of looking at it, so peaceful under a clear sky, and so dangerously rough when it wants to be threatening. When it is in this mood, I approach the jetty which joins up with the lighthouse, to watch its waves arrive with the speed of swift chargers, breaking with a crash against the rocks, making a burst of spray shoot upwards. It is a magnificent sight, before which we feel very small. In spite of my poor swimming skills, almost every morning I go and take advantage of the coolness of the water, which tones me up for the whole day.

XXV

Life is a beautiful gift. Why, then, was it taken away prematurely, from my godson Gil, and from my friend Jo, when they were at an age to know all its worth and were communicating it to others? With their exceptional gifts, and full of plans, they still had so much to give! ... While there are some people who drag out a long, drab existence, without sharing and without joy ... The feminine sensitivity of Anna de Noailles expresses the regret of it:

> Combien s'en sont allés de tous les coeurs vaillants
>> Au séjour solitaire
> Sans avoir bu le miel et respiré le vent
>> Des matins de la terre
> Ils n'ont pas répandu les essences et l'or
>> Dont leurs mains étaient pleines
> Les voici maintenant dans cette ombre où l'on dort
>> Sans rêve et sans haleine.

> (How many of these brave hearts have gone
>> To the lonesome dwelling place
> Not having drunk the honey nor inhaled the wind
>> Of earthly mornings
> They have not spread their essence nor their gold
>> With which their hands were full
> Now they are in those shadows where they sleep
>> Dreamless and unbreathing.)

It is only rich natures that can adorn life in society; each can exchange the joy of being for the joy of giving; a word of comfort, a smile – who can calculate the inestimable value of a smile? We are all in the same boat, tossing about at the wish of the forces of destiny, and we are unaware of the shipwrecks on our way. Let us endeavour then to make the crossing holding hands firmly, so that we can face adversity together.

'Go forth each morning, like Colombus for America, with wide, fresh eyes' advises our piquant southern writer Joseph Delteil. I try to emulate him, being naïvely intoxicated by the riches that life gives us so freely, and exhilarated at having the faculties with which to enjoy them: the scent and beauty of flowers, the cool freshness of the waters, the song of birds, the shade of the trees, the light of the sun...

We need to know how to vibrate to the beauty of things around us: how many Capestanais have gone into raptures over monuments and scenery of foreign countries and have never watched the setting sun gild the ancient stones of our *collégiale*, nor the reflection of our splendid plane trees in the green water of the canal? Each moment can be savoured: if we I know how to appreciate the little daily pleasures, the blue sky, a happy meeting, we will withstand better the disappointments of the day. But above all, it is the gift of self which is the source of happiness, the salvation in times of difficulty; I know from experience. I rejoice that I have preserved an enthusiastic and altruistic nature; I owe it certainly to all those who have been important in my life.

From time to time I go and visit my old haunts at Saint-Thibéry, and there I find myself back in familiar places in spite of all the changes that have taken place.

A new town made up of modern villas has been built on a hill overlooking the village. In bygone days it was unthinkable to plan dwellings on a piece of ground deprived of water, but recent techniques have accomplished the miracle.

This built-up area is without soul – that one must go and find in the old parts, which have kept their picturesque quality and the character of times gone by.

I am glad that my townsfolk's quality of life may be improved by large open spaces for relaxation, cultural halls, and the value which is placed on our heritage ... but my greatest pleasure is to wander in the streets, seeking out the surviving evidence of my youth. Reassured by the unchanged façade of my house, I wanted to see inside it again. The new owners were very proud to show me the transformations they had made.

'I congratulate you! It's very beautiful!' I couldn't disappoint them, but I no longer felt the warmth of the home where I had spent my adolescence. It made my heart break; everything had been turned upside down; the rooms enlarged to the detriment of familiar nooks and crannies, the luxury tiles, the sophisticated conversion killed my precious memories. I was a stranger in a house I did not know.

I took refuge in the home of my neighbour, the same age as myself, where I found again, with pleasure, all the old familiar things; the old-fashioned kitchen, and still by the fireplace, the cupboard where the sweets were kept, which used to be given to me whenever I came to visit . . . Is it possible that one should be so sensitive to these kinds of details?

After the shock which had upset me, this visit gave me back my confidence.

XXVI

Despite my loyalty to the village where I was born, Capestang is where I prefer to live. The hostility towards me at the beginning disappeared little by little, and I feel delightfully at home here. Over the years I have made close friendships with its inhabitants, and ties with the many associations whose dynamism is necessary to me. There are some tremendous young people who know all about the value of commitment, and put all their energy into serving the community.

Apart from the jubilant days of the Carnival and the local *fête* (celebrated differently from how it used to be but still drawing sizeable public participation), the favourite days of the Foyer Rural are the *fête* de Saint-Jean and the Craft Fair.

On 20th June, when night has fallen on the village, after a meal eaten by all the generations mingled together in the courtyard of the château, hands join up for a dance around an impressive bonfire. The most agile leap over the flames, then a band adds life to the evening and couples join up together until the early hours.

On the first Sunday in July, the town is animated throughout the day by the Craft Fair. From the early morning, the main thoroughfare of the village, from the church to the Place de l'Abreuvoir, is invaded by exhibitors who come from the region, and sometimes from further away (the Pays Basque and Limousin) . . . a wide range of products are on offer for the visitors' indulgence: honey, cheese, cider, wines, shellfish and many other gastronomic specialities; pottery stalls, sculpture, silks and various models line up against the façades of the houses. One can also have inscriptions or personalised motifs printed on articles of clothing, or choose novelty jewellery engraved with the name of the recipient. The artists have space set aside for them on the terrace and in the courtyard of the château.

The enthusiasts crowd into the Forum premises to the preview of an exhibition which must be the best of the year. This is also where the writers of the area meet up and sign their books.

There are many entertainments available for the crowd: a barrel organ churns out old familiar tunes from the past, the 'Wading-birds of the Vidourle' hold the crowd in thrall, a circle forms around a fire-eater, accompanied by acrobats and a juggler, while the harangue of a breaker of chains tries to attract the passers-by. In this atmosphere one would not be surprised to see a lady in medieval headdress ... There are some enjoyable little groups of musicians, and the *bandas* go playing through the streets or come to serenade the many guests who are sampling *cargolade*, grilled prawns, frogs' legs or seafood on the spot, washed down with plenty of good local wine.

It is always the occasion for a great public merry-making and good fun, which lasts until the evening.

In 1988, the Foyer Rural was able to achieve its aim of promoting an awareness of the local cultural heritage, and it knew how to arouse the interest of the majority of the village population around a project recalling an unhappy episode in Capestang's history. Entitled *The Republic of 1851*, a production was staged depicting the reactions of the republicans after the December *coup d'état*. It had been written with rare talent by Yves Vadot, a young teacher and actor with the Theatre de l'Impasse of Manosque, who was interested in the life of the village where he had spent some of his childhood. The mobilisation of the members of the secret societies, their resistance, their trial, the tortures in Guyana where some of them were deported, and the anxiety of the families were conveyed vividly and with much feeling. Ninety people were recruited to be involved in the production: actors, musicians, chorus singers, dancers: many of them braving the footlights for the first time, but they threw themselves into it with such heart and soul that they equalled their fellow players who were seasoned performers. For five consecutive evenings the audience took their places in the courtyard of the château, to

199

be immersed intensely in the drama of Jean Pech, a Capestanais devoted to justice and freedom, and his comrades. A rousing ovation from the audience every evening greeted his moving return to the country, accompanied by the singing of the chorus of slaves from *Nabucco*. It was a tremendous success which gave the necessary fillip to following up this sort of entertainment.

In 1991 the theatre group prepared a second venture which was about the Spanish immigration – an important event in the life of the village. Information was collected by those in charge at the Foyer during a trip to Spain, and evidence gleaned from witnesses amongst the village population was communicated to Yves Vadot who wrote the script for *Allà lejos*; Jo, who was chief of the orchestra and had already given his help in 1988, created the musical sequences, the songs and dances, which were accompanied by the local musicians. A succession of tableaux which depicted the locations and different eras, retraced the social struggles in Spain, the welcome in France, the inhuman treatment in the camps in the Pyrénées-Orientales, the hard and dangerous life in the Decazeville mines. The dramatically intense atmosphere of the work was happily tempered with comic, though always authentic, situations. Confident in the quality of the production, the audiences, often coming in from surrounding villages, crowded in for several evenings to the courtyard of the château.

The success of these two performances allowed Capestang to regain its theatrical tradition. This is to be rejoiced at for it is something which reveals talents, enables friendly exchange, and contributes to the cultural rebirth of the village.

At the same time, a society called 'L'Association du Sauvegarde du Patrimoine Naturel et Architectural de Capestang' was formed within the Foyer Rural, with the collaboration of certain eminent people who were very attached to the village. Its aim is to make accessible to the public the pictorial riches, neglected since the Middle Ages, which cover the ceiling of a room on the first floor of château. They were discovered fortuitously in 1976 in this crumbling place which had been used as an attic and had no longer been inhabited for years except by pigeons! Scenes of medieval life are depicted there:

courtly love, religious belief, diversions such as hunting, and also the fantasy world of those times: the fear of hell, grotesque grimacing faces, terrifying monsters ... These paintings are startlingly alive, they astonish with the freshness of their colours and constitute precious evidence of a rich past – justifying the interest of the publisher of *L'Imagier et ses Poètes* which has published reproductions:

'I was bowled over by the inspiration I felt on my visit to the château and its sumptuous *métopes*. I was encouraged to involve myself in this project after the wonderful welcome that I was given by the members of the Association de Sauvegarde du Patrimoine. They are exceptional people!'

The precarious site forbids access to these treasures, but help is being sought so that these marvels may soon be on view to the public, and so that their fame may enhance the renown of the village.

This same society is taking an interest in the evolution of the *étang*, which, alas, is the victim of pollution which is rampant everywhere, and no longer knows the abundance of its former life. In the course of Sunday outings, some members of the Foyer Rural go to study the habits of birds which still remain faithful to the environment of canes and reeds which sway over the still water. They respect their liberty, and it is from afar, in silence, that they observe their movements.

* * *

This refreshing new force eases my nostalgia for the past, for the bustle of our villages where all the trades mingled, the noise of their happy activity. The workshops are closed, and behind the heavy, silent portals, the tools sleep, from henceforth useless. Laughter used to burst forth from the little grocery where we used to go every day for a few purchases, but also to find out the local news relayed with humour and a certain spice of gossip.

Nowadays the housewives solemnly push their trolleys through the crowd, concerned about benefiting from the special offers in the supermarket, and collecting a bountiful supply of provisions.

There is no more whistling or singing in our streets: the artisans perched on their ladders listen to the racket which pours forth unceasingly at them from the transistors which follow them everywhere in their work.

In the countryside, one no longer hears the resonant commands of the men urging on their horses; these faithful companions of the peasant have disappeared; their slow tread no longer pounds the path through the vines. Only the throbbing of machines troubles the silence and frightens away the birds. When darkness falls and blurs the outlines, the streets are empty; one would think the village deserted ... but from each house bursts forth the echo of the television, and one can picture the family grouped round the magic box, some keen, some vacant, and often some asleep!

I apply to this magnificent discovery the epithet that someone once used to describe the tongue: 'The best and the worst of things!' This window opened onto the world brings a great deal of knowledge into our homes and is a valuable companion for people on their own. But it monopolises our attention, furthers a passive attitude and deprives us of enriching occupations. It is responsible for the lack of communication within families.

Seduced by an easy pleasure, the children succumb to its grip. I am distressed to see the young members of my family captivated by this leisure pursuit, often for mediocre reward.

Much though I rejoice in the facilities of present day life, liberated from a strict conformism and following the changing customs without too much reserve, I sometimes feel uneasy: I cannot get used to the dissonances of the music, certain sights disconcert me and I find no delight in the speed of travel on the autoroutes which lacks any romance. I feel out of step in certain circumstances: so, I am conscious of my ignorance, and of knowing next to nothing about modern technology when I see my grandchildren playing with the computer.

I am slightly appalled at the life style of our young families; the domestic tasks are simplified, but nevertheless they live at an exhausting pace.

I feel fortunate to have travelled the most part of my road through life in a period where we took our time to live. Our surrounds were narrower, but we developed in a climate of trust.

More and more, insecurity sets in and atrocities of various

kinds make us tremble for our children. My faith in human goodness sinks in the face of the violence committed in the world; we all moan about everything, but a general shock-start is needed for man to learn to respect life. 'La pensée qui n'est pas suivie d'action est une pensée morte.' (The thought which is not followed by action is a dead thought).

I admire the courage of young people, who live on the edge of a volcano; they have to struggle to be understood, to make themselves a place in society, and their leisure activities, which others judge to be excessive, often hide many fears.

Nowadays, families are broken up.

As far as I am concerned, I can't complain, as this dispersion gives me attractive prospects. The home of Nelly and Fausto, who are settled at Montpellier, is the nearest to my home, and I go there very enthusiastically, certain to have with Magali, Sarah and Maia a keen audience for my stories, my songs and my marionettes, which make me live time all over again.

Then, I visit Catalunia, where Remi and Simone's family give me a warm welcome. Mathieu is already a tall boy who is going to leave the *collège* directed by his father, to attend the *lyceé*, without neglecting his musical and sporting activities which he adores. Mireille's new home gives me the opportunity for numerous trips to Paris where I enjoy the attractions of the capital and unexpected privileges due to Patrick's position. It is my greatest joy to meet up with Numa again; he is an excellent sportsman who has succeeded in dragging me along on the ski slopes of Courcheval!

All my new descendants enrich and illumine the end of my life and I am profoundly grateful to them.

* * *

And so I have retraced my journey through life, without complacency, and in all sincerity. I have discovered that it has been dominated by two people whom I loved very much, who were very alike and who never met each other: my father and my husband.

With the former, a distance was imposed on me; I grew up at a time when parents had so much authority that a barrier existed between them and their children; one would never have dared to confide in them and this constraint is the cause of a great deal of misunderstanding; moreover the spirit of tenderness was restrained, and I have often asked myself if my father had any inkling of all the things I would have liked to express to him and if he was unsure of the place he occupied in my life. He left me when I was becoming adult and receptive ... a more intimate relationship would have enabled us to live some moments of privileged closeness. I was able to recapture this with my mother who shared my life for a long time.

Of my married life I regret nothing. It is true that with all his gifts, Emile could have aspired to a more shining destiny; but the simple life which he led in his familiar setting satisfied him. He was not burdened with any dishonest compromise, and he lived in complete freedom. I am happy to have had the means of sparing him any financial worries which he cared little about, and to have been able to collaborate in his artistic life. No other partner would have enriched me with such blossoming.

People are often astonished at my vitality and zest for life. I owe it to all the marvellous people who have accompanied me through it, to those who are no longer there, and to those who are here still; I pay tribute to them.

I have passed the normal span of life, but I am not yet spent. I still have an energy in me which only asks to be used and I have not finished exulting in the beauty of things. I see all my deficiencies and I would much like to make good some of them before my faculties slacken off. I owe this happy disposition to my environment. I have tasted all the pleasures and charm of living in this beautiful region, so blessed by nature. I have loved the sense of true values in my compatriots; here we take our time to live, but with the willingness to preserve the past, the better to prepare the future, and to be worthy of the rich traditions of our native land.

The roots of our vines are evidence of the permanence of the rhythm of the seasons and the continuance of life. They struggle against diseases and the effects of climate; their trunks become gnarled and tortured, but each year burst forth strong shoots, bearers of the plentiful harvest, source of gaiety and *joie de vivre*.

So too, in our book of life, are written down, day after day,

musical phrases in different keys, sometimes major, sometimes minor. The flats and sharps jostle one another there
according to the circumstances of our journey. It is up to us to
conduct this symphony, with the faith of an honest heart, to
retain only the clear and vibrant melody, and to make of it a
centre of joy which does not give up hope in humanity.

André Maurois said:

'Vieillir est une mauvaise habitude
L'homme occupé n'a pas le temps de la prendre.'

(To grow old is a bad habit
Which the busy man has not time to acquire.)

I confess that I have not yet succumbed to it.

February 1994.

GLOSSARY

abreuvoir: watering place, drinking trough.
à l'affenage: tied up, tethered.
Alla lejòs: what we have left behind. (Sp)
allez huc: Gee up!
amandes des dames: a variety of almond, easier to open.
amandes noisettes: another variety of almond, smaller and
  rounder.
andouillettes: little sausages made of pork chitterlings
  (intestines).
anisette: a liquorice-flavoured liqueur, made from aniseed.
aramon: a grape which was grown extensively in the area. Of
  inferior quality for wine making, but very disease-resistant,
  and imparting a deep red colour to the wine.
L'Arlésienne: 'The Girl from Arles'.
**Association du Sauvegarde du Patrimoine Naturel et
  Architectural de Capestang**: Association for the
  Preservation of the Natural and Architectural Heritage of
  Capestang.
aux moules frais: Come, buy fresh mussels!
avis à la population: Notice to the people (Oyez! Oyez!)
azerolles: small rosy fruit which grow on a tree. Rather like
a miniature cherry, with a tiny stone in the middle.

baccalauréat: secondary school examination giving university
  entrance qualification.
battoir: a wooden beater.
berlingots: boiled sweets, humbugs.
bombe glacée: an ice-cream dessert.
bon coup de fourchette: a good meal (a lucky forkful).
Le Bordelais: The man from Bordeaux.

boudin: a blood sausage.
bouillabaisse: fish soup.
bouilli: stew slowly simmered with vegetables.
Bourbonnais: Bourbons.
bourgeois: Middle class, comfortably off.
bourgeoisie: the middle class.
bourride: a fish stew.
bouteillous: (Occ) water containers, bottles.
Boutonnet: a district in the north of Montpellier, where the Ecole Normale was situated.
Brevet supérieur: an examination which used to be taken at about the age of 16–17, roughly similar to O-level.
bucheuses: the girls who thought of nothing else but their school work – 'swots'.
bugadières: (Occ) washerwomen.

café au lait: coffee with milk.
café d'un sou: a cheap café.
caillé: junket.
canottes: tall canes.
cargolade: a dish of snails.
carnaval: Carnival, also the Carnival King.
carte d'alimentation: ration card.
casseröles: fast fairground whirligigs with revolving bucket seats.
cassoulet: a regional dish from S.W. France, made from beans, sausage, pork, lamb etc., cooked slowly.
Catalunia: Catalonia – region of N.E. Spain with a strong separatist tradition.
causerie: talk, chat.
cave: cellar.
caves-cooperatives: wine cooperatives.
châpeau de printemps: spring hat.
charcuterie: cooked pork meats; a shop selling these.
cloches: bells; legend has it that the church bells flew to Rome for Holy Week, and returned full of Easter eggs, which were scattered in their joyful ringing.
Club du 3me Age: Senior Citizens' Club.
cochonailles: products of the pig.
collabos: collaborators.

colle: group which makes up a team of grape-pickers.

collège: secondary school for pupils up to the age of 15–16.

collégiale: collegiate church.

comportes: wooden carriers for the grapes.

cortège: funeral procession.

correspondants: correspondents – people who were in regular business contact with one another in other parts of the country.

côtelettes: chops.

couvent: convent.

Dame Tartine: character in an old French nursery rhyme, who had a house made from many different kinds of sweetmeats.

demi-deuil: half mourning.

deputé: member of the French Parliament.

dominos: eye masks worn in masquerades, carnivals, etc.

douleurs: pains.

école laïque: state school, unattached to any religious denomination.

école maternelle: infant school.

école normale: Primary-School Teachers' Training College.

école primaire-supérieure: Secondary School.

écu: a crown.

en manque: deprived, lacking in.

entrées: starters.

envahissement: invasion.

escargot: snail.

étang: pond, mere; in the case of Capestang's 'etang', a large expanse of marshland and water.

examen des bourses: bursary exam.

examen saboté: sabotaged exam.

faire tapisserie: to make wallpaper (lit). i.e., to be a wallflower.

farandole: a lively dance from Provence in four-four time.

fatigue du cochon: (pig duty) – the task of killing the pig and making the resulting pig-products.

fer à glacé: goffering iron.

Fernandel: (real name Fernand Joseph Desire Contadin) 1903–1971. French comic film actor.

Festival de la Côte Languedocienne: Festival of the Languedoc Coast.

fête: celebration, party, saint's day.

fête de l'amicale: party for the Association of Friends (of the Ecole Normale).

fête de la déscente: party to celebrate the over-halfway stage in the students' studies.

fête de retour: welcome back party.

fête de St Jean: St John the Baptist's Day.

fil chinois: an extremely strong sewing thread. Collecting the paper wrappings from round the spools enabled one to send them off to the manufacturers after a certain number had been amassed, and a 'present' would be sent in return.

fonctionnaires: civil servants, employees of the state.

fougasse: left-over dough shaped in a lattice pattern and baked as bread.

fouloir: wine press.

Foyer Rural: hostel, village hall association, youth club, etc.

fromage du table: inexpensive everyday cheese for the table.

garrigue: hilly, rocky scrubland between plain and mountains.

gigot: leg of lamb.

grandes écoles: prestigious schools of university level with competitive entrance examinations, e.g. Ecole Polytechnique.

grande lessive: the big wash.

gratins: cheese-topped dishes.

halles: covered markets.

harmonie: wind band, wind ensemble.

hectolitre: one hundred litres.

impasse: cul de sac.

jeux taurins: sport or games of various kinds involving bulls or heifers.

jour de fête: holiday, feast day.

laitières: dairy women.
Languedoc: the region of southern France lying between the foothills of the Pyrénées and the river Rhone.
leur verte vieillesse: their (ever)green old age.
Lézignan onion: a speciality of Lezignan and its surrounds, this onion has a particularly sweet and juicy flavour.

madeleines: little sponge cakes.
mairie: the town hall, centre of the town or village administration.
maisons de maîtres: gentlemen's residences.
Maman: Mother.
manque de sérieux: lack of responsibility.
Marchal: Marshal (in this case, Marshal Pétain).
marchand d'oublis: an itinerant pedlar, selling small cones of unconsecrated communion wafer, which were drawn from his barrel.
Marchand de sable: Mr Sandman.
Marseillaise: the French national anthem.
meneuse: leader of the female grape-pickers.
métopes: friezes.
meunières: millers' wives.
minet boit son lait: pussy drinks her milk.
musique adoucit les moeurs: music breaks down barriers.
musique de droit; musique de gauche: right wing music; left wing music.

Noirot: an extract, supplied in very small bottles, used in making liqueur.
notaire: lawyer, solicitor.
nounours: teddy bear.
nouveaux riches: people who have recently acquired wealth and are regarded as vulgarly ostentatious.

Occitan: the 'langue d'oc' – the language of Provençal France.
omelettes flambées: omelettes served in flaming brandy.
opaline: an opaque whitish glass.
oreillettes: small, sweet, 'ear'-shaped cakes made into rings and fried.

pâtés de Pézénas: tiny sweetmeats made of fine pastry filled with a special sweet filling.

Pays d'Oc: the area in which the Occitan language is spoken.

pâtisserie: cake shop, confectioners.

pâquerettes: daisies – here the noun has been 'conjugated' as a verb.

patron: the boss, owner.

pech: a hill.

petit pain de tortosa: a sweetmeat made of very strong liquorice.

pinguoins: penguins.

place: a town or village square.

plat de résistance: main course.

poissonnerie: fishmonger's shop or stall.

poilus: a French soldier in the First World War.

pompiers: firemen.

pot-au-feu: a stew.

précon: town crier.

quicheur: the man who crushes the grapes down into the comporte.

ragoûts: meat stews.

raisiné: a thick sweet liquid made from the pulp, skin and seeds of the grapes.

rendez-vous: meeting, tryst.

repas: a meal.

repounchous: (Occ) a wild plant with edible roots, like a very small radish.

sans-culottes: the humorous meaning here is 'without knickers' and comes from the time of the French Revolution when the revolutionaries wore pantaloons or trousers rather than knee breeches.

sangria: a Spanish drink of red wine, sugar, orange or lemon juice, and iced soda, sometimes laced with brandy.

saquette: little bag containing food for the midday meal.

seaux: buckets.

Sirène de l'Etang: siren of the lake.

sou: shilling.

souches: vine stocks, roots, vine stumps.

souillard: storeroom, scullery.

souquets: little bits pruned from the vine stumps.

tableau: a scene (theatrical).

tellines: tiny bivalves collected in the wet sand along the shore line.

tourtes: pastry flans.

tutoie: 'tutoyer' – to use the familiar 'tu' instead of 'vous' when speaking to someone, thereby expressing being on more familiar terms.

une année d'avance: having to pay for things a year in advance of the harvest.

vendanges: the grape harvest.

vendangeurs: grape pickers and harvest workers.

vesces: a type of wild vetch, used as fodder.

vigneron: wine grower who makes his own wine on the property.

viticulteur: wine grower who sends his grapes to the cooperative.

vous: addressing someone in the second person plural, used in all conversation except when people are on very familiar terms, as would be the case between parents and children.